EMBODYING THE DIVINE MASCULINE
of All Truth

THROUGH THE HIGH PRIEST

By
Carmel Glenane B.A. Dip. Ed.

EMBODYING THE DIVINE MASCULINE
of All Truth

THROUGH THE HIGH PRIEST

By
Carmel Glenane B.A. Dip. Ed.

Big Country Publishing, LLC

Embodying The Divine Masculine of All Truth, Through The High Priest
©2016 by Carmel Glenane B.A. Dip. Ed.
ISBN: (print) 978-1-938487-25-5
ISBN: 978-1-938487-26-2 (eBook)
Library of Congress Control Number: 2016941011
Portions taken from the original publication *"The High Priest"* ©2010 by Carmel Glenane.
ID20682421 ©Nightman1965 dreamstime.com
ID47155923 ©Milan Petrovic dreamstime.com

All rights reserved. No part of this publication may be reproduced, stored in a retrieval system, or transmitted, in any form or by any means electronic, mechanical, photocopying, recording, or otherwise without prior written permission from the publisher except in the case of brief quotations embodied in critical articles and reviews.

The author and publisher of the book do not make any claim or guarantee for any physical, mental, emotional, spiritual, or financial result. All products, services, and information provided by the author are for general education and entertainment purposes only. The information provided herein is in no way a substitute for medical or other professional advice. In the event you use any of the information contained in this book for yourself, the authors and publisher assume no responsibility for your actions. Big Country Publishing, LLC accepts no responsibility or liability for any content, bibliographic references, artwork, or works cited contained in this book.
Published by Big Country Publishing, LLC 7691 Shaffer Parkway, Suite C Littleton, CO 80127 USA www.bigcountrypublishing.com

Printed in the United States of America, United Kingdom, and Australia
Books may be ordered through booksellers or by contacting: Atlantis Rising Healing Centre P.O. Box 376, Coolangatta, QLD, 4225 Australia
www.carmelglenane.com www.atlantis-rising.com.au
www.senjukannonreiki.com +61 (0) 7 55 367 399

Because of the dynamic nature of the Internet, any web addresses or links contained in this book may have changed since publication and may no longer be valid.

TABLE OF CONTENTS:

Note from the Author 7
Acknowledgements 9

Part I: All Truth 11
Introduction to All Truth 13

Part II: The High Priest 77
Introduction to the High Priest 79

Chapter 1   The High Priest Speaks 83
Chapter 2   Connecting with The High Priest 95
Chapter 3   Ptah, The Ancient Egyptian God 109
Chapter 4   Attuning to The High Priest 125
Chapter 5   Identify with your High Priest 139
Chapter 6   Activating your Immortality 149
Chapter 7   The Divine Masculine 157

Part III: The High Priest Lessons 171
Lesson One   Emotions 173
Lesson Two   Shifting Your Reality 181

Lesson Three	Enacting the Masculine Principle 189
Lesson Four	The Vibration of the High Priest 197
Lesson Five	Your Creative Force 207
Lesson Six	Opening up to Your Consciousness 213
Lesson Seven	Universal Heart Frequency 217

About the Author 223
Meditations by Carmel Glenane 225
Other Books by Carmel Glenane 229
Tours and Events with Carmel Glenane 235

Note from the Author

In this book, "Embodying the Divine Masculine of All Truth Through the High Priest," you will be a witness to your own power to change your reality through your own inner masculine. You will receive the powerful tool and rituals for giving yourself back your own mighty magic. The concept of All Truth is a new frequency opening up your multidimensionality. Enacting it is as simple as turning on a light switch. Try it.

All Truth brings ancient sacred laws to you and these laws are invisible forces that bring power to your whole totality. Feeling this now brings you closer to the essence and heart of yourself.

Within the teachings of The High Priest, you will understand how to take control of your creative masculine. The High Priest offers a practical guide to living powerfully, with truth, changing your definition of your current reality.

Allow yourself your truth through power, to bring protection, power and love!

Heart I Love You,
Carmel

ACKNOWLEDGEMENTS

I acknowledge the sacred forces through the Divine Masculine to shape my life.

Through the power of the balanced masculine I have expanded my awareness of my totality bringing light, power and peace.

The masculine vibration is felt everywhere as a force of creation.

I acknowledge the source of the creative masculine in the sun every day and the principle of life behind the sun.

Through the magician Priests of the Ancient World whose awesome presence was a sight to behold, I thank you.

All sentient and non-sentient beings who have shaped my multi-dimensional self, I give to you my gratitude.

The Mother's story through her son is a gift to your intelligent heart.

Allow yourself to receive the Divine Masculine through the great Mother.

Carmel Glenane

Introduction to All Truth

Right now this transmission allows the force of truth to be heard, felt, seen, touched and tasted in human consciousness.

For what is a human life if truth cannot be enacted? Why would a human journey not want a truth-filled experience? We are born wanting truth and truth keeps us safe; keeping safe brings light and an invisible shield is placed around us.

The All Truth guides are supervising this work. The All Truth guides comprise a group of ascended beings that carry a vibration of order, justice, peace and light.

Your journey with these energy "beings" begins now as you embrace and embody the Divine Masculine of All Truth Through The High Priest.

Part I:
All Truth

Truth is a way of expressing your humanness in a way which allows a state of *grace* to be enacted. A state of grace is conferred upon those seeking truth.

Many things shape your identity: The greatest shaper of *identity* is *truth*. Why? Truth shapes the vibration of "All Love." When we love All and bring All into the experience of loving, we need a guiding companion. Truth is such a companion.

This identity brings with it a true purpose and meaning in being human and allowing this true purpose to carve out a meaningful life. A meaningful life has order encoded in it. A meaningful life has love and respect for all living things. When we respect all living things we become one with all living things. You are now carving out a pattern of existence that has this value encoded in it. Life allows for the experience of being truthful every single moment we give power and discipline to anything.

Power and discipline bring light, order and peace. You are embodying peace, light and order when you summon All Truth to be part of your cellular remembering.

When we experience a truth-filled life, all of life responds. All of life responds to the call of truth, and the way of truth is the way of power, light and love.

As you embark on this journey, you are finding within yourself now, the essence of your remembering. You are finding now that All Truth speaks of a power in your life you have previously not encountered. This power shifts consciousness not only in yourself but on the planet as well.

Allowing this shift of consciousness brings to you a sense of absoluteness for everything. Why is this energy so important to our planet earth right now? It is important to allow this sense of power and light to come to you; your consciousness has encoded in it all you ever were and all you ever will be. Just focusing on this power now brings with it a subtle but powerful vibration: You are forwarding the essence of this power when you are alive to the mystery. Being alive to the mystery brings with it a sense of pure absoluteness for every living thing; you are vibrating to this energy right now. This energy has encoded in it a sense of power and light.

Power and light bring a sense of truth. Truth and power go together. Truth and power create with you now in a way you cannot imagine: Giving power back to yourself when you are fearful is enacting truth. Truth brings order: Truth brings absoluteness. You are feeling now the power and strength of truth create a shift in your head. This is a shifting of energy; of consciousness. Feeling this now brings power, light and even more truth to you.

Bringing truth as a vibration to any situation brings the heart into enactment of ritual. Ritual, all ritual, set the pattern for truth to be enacted and truth being enacted creates space and order for the mystery to unfold.

When you begin to perceive your life as having truth encoded in it, you begin to allow yourself to create with this special remembering. You are creating with this special remembering every time you allow your own energy; essence and life force create with you. You are allowing your own identity to shape itself in a new and powerful way. This enactment creates in it a sense of knowing that you and life are one. You and life are creating with this "one" now: You and life are resonating with the "one." You are allowing "the one." "The one" of everything brings you to the state of special magic for all there is. Allowing this magical essence to enfold you now brings a sense of power and light for all there is.

The sense of power and light for all there is creates in you a sense of absoluteness for all there is. Absoluteness for all there is, brings "the all" of everything to every situation, concept and relationship you are manifesting at any time. Allowing this special space to envelope you creates in you a sense of reverence and stillness for all of life. All of life and you are one. You are all of everything now. All and you are one.

Believing in your own ability to trust in the special relationship with "All Truth" allows you to tap into a gold mine of power. Power creates respect; power and respect go hand in hand.

When power is enacted, truth becomes manifested in your very being. This vibration sets up a pattern, a pattern of light and power in all you ever were and will be. You are opening up now to truth as being a "power" keg for you now as you allow "you," truth to become manifest.

For power brings an inner beauty to a person. Power brings *light* and power brings a sense of *dignity*. A person who embodies "All Truth" just embodies a special aspect of her or himself that goes beyond any previous definition of what it is to be human.

There is a sense of allowance in you now, as this space is being made ready for you. Allowing this magical space to be made ready for you brings you to a space of resonance for all there is. Feeling this space allows you to tap into a sense of wonder and power for all there is. This magical reverence has encoded in it peace, light and beauty. For what are we if we cannot be totally truthful to ourselves? What are we if we cannot allow ourselves to manifest with this truth-filled state?

This truth-filled state creates magic, peace and wonder for all of life. All of life is recreated in this truth-filled space. You are one in essence with this vibration now.

Allowing truth to create with you brings to you a sense of peace. A peace-filled state begins to become a way of life; truly, a peace-filled peaceful space becomes an inner haven, not only for yourself but it is a shelter for all who are in your presence. This is very powerful. This power brings with it a sense of dignity, peace and light for all there is. This sense of peace, space and dignity creates in you a sense of true purpose for all there is as well. Allowing your own special relationship to develop with yourself brings power to you right now. This power has encoded in it order, peace and light.

Order, peace and light bring divine alchemy into your being. You are witnessing yourself as being part of creation itself, part of the web of life. Allowing this web of life to create with you allows you now to partake in the mystery. The mystery of having all you ever were become one with you. Just focusing on this vibration brings to you now a sense of trust and truth for all there is. Trust and truth for all there is allows you, your own sacred essence and power to become one with all there is and all there ever will be.

Power to the light of your divinity within creates a sense of absoluteness for every living thing. Absoluteness for every living thing creates in you the essence of every living thing: We are all as humans divine beings as well. All we are is vibration at different levels of evolution and experience. Chaotic forces are balanced when we consider this level of vibration to support our evolution.

Believing in the forces of light to trust truth allows the sacred flow of the vibration of truth to be your guide. You are allowing these sacred forces to create with you every moment you allow the essence, energy and life force of every living thing create with you. The essence, energy and life force brings a magical intent, one of absoluteness in everything. Everything has absoluteness encoded in it and everything is absolute.

The force and energy that comes with absoluteness bring even more power and light, opening up your whole being to the force of its power. Allowing this force, this energy to manifest with you brings you into the heart of the mystery. The mystery has encoded in it truth for the absolute essence of whom you are; the absolute essence of your magical life force, light and spirit.

This flow, this essence, this light magnifies all around you with the magical essence of all you ever were. All you ever were, is a sum total of "All" in everything.

"I am 'The All' of everything."

"All" radiates through me, and "All" is in me. 'The All' of who I am, is just that: 'All'; 'All'; 'All'."

"All Truth" is the sum total of all truth-filled experiences vibrationally. The vibration takes care of all fear that comes through you as a space of negativity coming within you and through you. You are the sum total of it all and "The All" of truth creates this power and energy.

Believing in the essence, energy and light of your truth allows the magnification of truth to surround you. Right now you are being re-attuned yourself, for the vibration of "All Truth" to encode itself upon your cellular matrix.

Your cellular matrix is one of pure peace and power for all there is. This pure peace and power allow the force of magical love to surround you.

The force of magical love allows the spirit and love of your own light and power to bring you all you need to create a world of absoluteness for everything. Everything creates through you and in you, everything creates in the essence of all there is. Everything brings with it, the sum total of all there ever was and will be. The essence of "All Truth" brings to you this sense of absoluteness for it all.

Allowing the secret essence of your magical heart to envelope you brings down source energy and light. Source energy and light encodes itself on you now as you create a world of pure love and trust for the process of being human. The process of being human just creates in you all there ever was, and all there ever will be. The allowance of this energy brings with it magical power and intent for all there is. Allowing the forces of the world to create with you brings magic and life to you.

You are one in this essence, energy and magic now. Creating with it brings power, truth and light. You are allowing this reality to shape your belief in truth for all there is. Truth for all there is brings magic for all there is. Allowing the force of "All Truth" to envelope you now, brings more power. "All Truth" brings power.

You are witnessing right now the complete acceptance of "All Truth" as a way of being human and one with all there is. You are allowing the special magic of your own humanness to guide you now, and deliver you the absoluteness of being human. The absoluteness of being human has encoded in it a respect and acknowledgement for all there is and a knowing that all there is brings you to the point of truth for the mystery.

You are creating with the mystery and the power and might of your own divinity. Your own divinity brings with it source raw power, the primordial power of all life, for "All Truth" rests in this primordial power and essence, of all life. Allowing this energy to bring you your own love and truth allows the secret sacred self to create with you. The essence of the vibration of this power allows for truth and light to be one with you.

The black, luminous power rests in this vibration. You are "absoluting" in this energy. You are "absoluting" in this power. This power is so great that you must be careful how you use it. For it strikes, it knows the force, which attacks it, the darkness within the soul, and strikes at this force with the weapon of the destruction, which started the dark force in the first place. This force is just there, and is known by the dark: The dark knows this force, and this force dissolves the denser dark intelligence.

"All Truth" creates in you now a sense of truth for all life. All life has truth encoded in it, and "All Truth" has light encoded in it. The essence of "All Truth" and light brings you to a point of absoluteness for all there is. The point of absoluteness for all there is, is in allowing the force of absoluteness as an energy to create with you a special relationship with "All" there is. The special relationship with "All" there is allows the light and truth of spirit to merge with you in a way of celebration. There is a feeling of celebration for your journey right now, and this feeling of celebration has encoded in it a sense of really knowing who and what you are, and why you are here.

You are here as a human to celebrate your creation with all you are capable of in being in a body with an intelligence to create peace in you and your world. What you are witnessing in yourself now is a drawing down of this spirit, and a truth and trust in this spirit as well. Truth and trust in this spirit of truth, keeps you safe and keeps you free. Free to trust and be free. Trust and freedom bring to your world this magic and energy. This magic and energy allow you, the energy of "you" to celebrate and renew yourself in this energy. Celebrating and renewing yourself in this energy creates a sense of wonder for all there is. Celebrate your union with "All Truth" now.

It truly is a gift for yourself and your humanity right now. The gift of your love of "All Truth" brings with it profound love and peace for all there is. Profound love and truth for all there is, allows magic and light to encode you. All encodements, all love and all light create magic and truth for the process of being human. You are feeling this energy and power now. Celebrate this gift in you beingness now.

"All Truth" is the sum total of "All" in truth. Truth is not spoken to anyone (like honesty); it is spoken to you. The truth in "All Truth" means to be truthful to your heart.

Being truthful to your heart is the sum total of "All Truth."

You are witnessing the core aspect of yourself now creating with "All Truth." This essence has encoded in it your own ability to create a world, which has truth as part of the core mystery. You are witnessing truth being enacted all the time you are allowing yourself to speak to your heart, which reflects your own ability to create complete cellular destruction and creation of a heart that responds to truth. This is a time to really feel free, now the essence of truth in everything. Every living thing has truth encoded in it.

Animals, birds, nature all have "All Truth" encoded in their cellular matrix, they just are truthful to their species. A lion kills its prey; the prey knows it will be hunted; the bird knows it can fly; dolphins will kill; this is called the law of nature. Humans do not have this coding; this is "All Truth" for us as a species. As a species, we are not truthful to our own species, because humans have come from many different colonies and planetary evolutions and civilizations. We come to learn to love our own karmas and off-earth civilizations traits come into play, making being human, jungle life.

Our own emotional patterns untrained are our biggest enemy. Our own intelligence is pitted against us in terms of being truthful to ourselves and those who live with us on the planet.

Feeling this and understanding it brings you closer to understanding why "All Truth" is essential for humans to live harmoniously with each other. Feeling the essence of "All Truth" creates a sense of order in yourself, where you are not a victim to your emotional self. The emotional self is an enemy of a truth-filled way of being human.

You are now feeling the power of "All Truth" making "you" the "star," the "product."

How can "All Truth" become realized in human consciousness?

It becomes realized in human consciousness when it is embodied in the person, and the person is you.

You must see yourself on the pages:
 "Yes, this is what I want to embody; this is my truth."

You cannot market a philosophy, a business or a dream unless it is "you"; "you" are the personality embodying the product; "All Truth" and what it will give you.

So ask yourself now:
 What will "All Truth" as a way of being human, give me?

I want to feel it and experience it before I say I embody it.

Right now ask yourself;
 Would I like to embody "All Truth?"

You may like to get a pen and paper and write it down:
 "I now experience with "All Truth," "Power."

"All Truth" brings power against my emotional self. "All Truth" brings power.

Do you like the idea of being powerful?

Creating with "All Truth" brings responsibility, not only to yourself, but how you create in your world. You cannot be separate from who "you" are. You cannot dictate to another what you are incapable of embodying yourself.

This is why we now have leaders and politicians not trusted; they aren't "truthful" to themselves. Humanity has changed; it has now encoded in it a more intuitive way of observing others now, and as a species we are parting the veil on illusion created by others in the name of leadership.

Your life is now one of just observing how truthful our species is to each other. Observing our own truth brings with it a sense of absoluteness for every living thing. Absoluteness for every living thing has encoded in it the essence and value of truth. Right now you are allowing the essence and value of truth to create with you all you ever were, and all you ever will be. It's right now that you make the decision to be truth filled and to live and create with "All Truth" as a way of being human.

This allowance is one of surrender. Surrender to the forces of truth around you brings to you "All Truth." Surrendering to "All Truth" brings a sense of absoluteness in everything. Absoluteness creates in you a sense of absolute totality for the reflection of the moment as being just that. Perfect. The perfection of truth is that it cannot be compromised once it has been cemented into human consciousness; it is wired in, hard wired. It creates solidity and order.

Feeling the power of "All Truth" creates in you now the essence of absoluteness in everything. Feeling the power of "All Truth" is an enactment of mystery. The enactment of mystery brings power, light and magic to your life right now. For you cannot go anywhere but inside yourself right now.

You cannot allow the past to dominate you anymore. You are one in essence with this power now as you begin to feel the manifestation of "All Truth" in your cellular memory. Every breath is an act of remembrance of your power to remember this truth and live it. This is an enactment of power and truth for the mystery. The enactment of power and truth for the mystery brings with it the sense of absoluteness for all there is.

Right now you are feeling this power and you are beginning to witness yourself as an all-loving being creating in the vibration of truth. Surrendering to truth brings truth seekers to you, not needy fools who want to trap you. You are witnessing now your vibration of "All Truth." The feeling of truth brings with it a rare sense of ownership of yourself right now; a rare sense of the spirit of ownership is now yours. Allow the magic and essence of truth to be your guide, shaping your identity and power. Power is the weapon! The Goddess is the weapon for a truth-filled way of being, as you carve out your power to summon "All Truth."

"All Truth" is a manifestable energy, because it brings a vibration of complete surrender to everything. The power of the manifestable energy is very strong in you now as you create truth and abundance.

Your ability to create abundance is measured by the energy of truth and light you carry. The energy of truth and light brings with it peace, space and light. Your vibration is matching "All Truth" as a manifestable thing. The essence of manifestation brings with it power and light. Power and light transform energy and it is through truth that you are able to allow yourself all you need for your life or power. For truth brings power; mighty power. Truth carries a vibration so great that it blasts away all fear of limitation and loss. *How can there be loss when the almighty force of truth is the reward?* The reward for truth is power. The gift of power brings energy; energy and power are one. There is a sense of absoluteness when energy and power are creating with you.

This is time to allow this sense of energy and power to be yours. You are vibrating to the sense of this energy and power now as truth becomes encoded in you. The essence of truth being encoded in you brings power and truth. Allow the force of truth and power to create all you need right now. They are your weapons, and you must feel free to create with these weapons. Allowing truth to be your guide brings power, truth and light. Light and truth are one. Light, truth and power create with you now. You are the essence of this almighty force now.

"All Truth" now comes to you to strengthen yourself to fight against your own emotional reactions against the tyranny of your own emotional heart and mind. Mental health is being created through a mind that won't be disciplined. This is an absolutely essentially important time in your own evolution and your species evolution, to get the power balance back, so at least more light can be poured into you.

The planet needs more people who are truth seeking to really lift the veil off patterns of fear; loss and distrust around allowing enough light to balance the darkness your planet is experiencing right now. This energy; this force allows you now to really create a world of absoluteness in everything in your life right now.

The essence, the force, the magic, the truth is just such an unbelievable force right now. The essence of "All Truth" as a force is one of the almightiest energies to create with. The energy of creation creates with this force. "All Truth" brings the force, the power, the light and the will to create with every living thing.

Every living thing can be called upon in its pure essential form to create this magic with you now. The magic of your resurrection of spirit over the density of matter: Mind over matter, brings power. The mind is an almighty weapon. However, the heart once it is awakened to its full intelligence is even greater!

The full intelligence is never fully awakened until the heart, the Immortal Heart is awakened to "All Truth," as "All Truth" smashes the skull, the mind of its power to limit your total consciousness.

To create with "All Truth" requires a belief in all you are capable of. You are bringing the senses of this energy to your light body now as you plunge deeper and deeper into your core remembering. This core remembering seeds your own belief in yourself as an immortal being.

You are allowing yourself now to smash all illusions about what you can and cannot have in your life. Your essence goes to another dimension. Your essence goes to the space of power and light for all there is. Your essence creates a space for this growth now. Feeling the essence of your life brings you now a sense of true remembering for your power to receive. That essence is one of trust for all there is, and brings with it all you were. All you ever were is in the allowance of "All Truth" to create power, magic and light.

You are focusing more and more on having truth-filled people around you, and there is a feeling of complete detachment from your need to support others at the expense of yourself.

This is a time for powerful remembering. This remembering has encoded in it the absolute essence of all there ever was, and all there ever will be. Finding this sense of absoluteness brings a sense of refined power and light to you. Simple power and light reinforces more power and light and you are vibrating to the sense of absoluteness in everything now.

"I am allowing this true sense of power and light to be mine now. I am love."

"All Truth" brings an enormous sense of raw transformative power to you. When "All Truth" becomes enacted the raw power source energy just becomes available to you. You are connecting to this sense of raw power now as the mysteries reveal themselves to you. You are vibrating to this now, as your power and light become one in the essence of all life. To feel the essence of all life through "All Truth" allows you to create with the mysteries.

Creating with the mysteries brings to you the source energy of "All Truth." "All Truth" and you are one. You're opening the fire energy now in the full aspect of the Tantra. For the true Tantra is the union with this flame; this is the "Blue Flame" of truth: You are allowing this "Blue Flame" to create with you now.

The ascension of "All Truth" through your central core matrix brings with it a sense of raw power and light for the mysteries. The essence of the mysteries is enacting the power of the Tantra, the Egyptian Sa Sekhem Sahu.

You are summoning this power source when you open up to the source energy of all life, and you are enacting mystery with it too. Right now the essence, energy and life force bring to you the source energy of this power and mystery. This energy essence and life force has for you the expression of all life encoded in it. The expression of all life brings to you truth for the mystery. Allowing the precious energy of a life to create with you is in allowing the portal to really open in your cellular remembering. Bring this power and light through the "Blue Flame"; the blue fire of truth; Truth: "All Truth" is the master. Now is the time to strike a blow for truth and allow you to create with the mystery. You are creating with the mysteries all the time you bring to your world your essence, energy and light. You are finding your own power and strength now in enacting truth and you must really allow the essence, energy and life force to bring you now a sense of absoluteness for every living thing. This is a time to allow the mystery to unfold and reveal itself to you, for you are allowing the secret sacred self to emerge.

This secret sacred self has its core in the very being of your cellular remembering. Right now, your cellular remembering has encoded in it a sense of true power and ownership of all you ever were. All you ever were brings with it a sense of raw power and energy for the mysteries. The essence of the mysteries lies in enactment of truth.

Truth is the greatest enactor of the mysteries. Truth is the glue that binds the universe together. Truth is the power source, which fuels the rocket of the universes. The full power of truth cannot be measured in the knowledge humans have about themselves at this moment. You are vibrating now to the key of the universe. "All Truth" unlocks the secrets of it all.

How can I use this in a daily way?

Firstly: Earth it.

And get three key phrases:

"The secret sacred self emerges with 'All Truth.'"
"Truth is the glue that binds the universe."
"I am vibrating now to the keys of the universe."

Feeling the presence of truth is a sensuous experience. The sensuousness of truth is in activating the heart's intelligence to receive the masculine counterpart of the feminine remembering.

The Feminine remembers.
The Masculine creates through the remembering.
The essence of remembering and the creative birthing of it, through "All Truth" create the essence of power and light for illumination of the heart's truth. You are a witness to this remembering now as you birth your heart's truth.

See, hear, taste, touch and smell truth as a calling to activate the love. The love is activated. The "self love" is now awake. "All Truth" is the messenger. All you are truthful about is what your heart wants. My heart wants to receive love, to live in a human body and develop its consciousness in that body. You must seek to activate this cellular remembering right now. Seeking to address this remembering and creating with it is what "All Truth" is about. Very simple really!

A baby awakens; it cries for nourishment and the need to survive. Its guardian is truth. Its screams are screams of truth. *"Yes, help me. I am hungry, cold, frightened."*

We must always honor the need for truth in our lives by monitoring all cries for help our heart gives us and get those needs met, lovingly, respectfully, but immediately.

This is the simple essence of what "All Truth" is. It is a very simple message indeed.

See, hear, taste, touch and smell truth. Tell your heart's senses now:

* Truth is the masculine activator to the heart's feminine need to experience love.

* "All Truth" is just listening to my "All Love" heart and delivering the goods.

* We must always honor the need for truth in our lives, by monitoring all cries for help.

Loving the sense of power to create magic brings to you now the essence of every living thing as you complete yourself and bring to yourself the entirety of your true heart. *The true heart wants peace, bliss and, above all, wants to feel loved.*

Every human on the planet from the richest to the poorest; from the greatest spiritual guru to the darkest human all only want to be loved. They are craving for recognition. Recognition from the source of "self" love not through other people brings the greatest and most almighty power to you. *The greatest living energy is the power of the individual to love "themselves," completely.*

You are witnessing now the birth of yourself in a truth-filled way, one of complete acceptance of yourself in this new form. This new form has encoded complete love and truthfulness in it. Complete love and truthfulness brings order, peace and love. Order, peace and love are the catalyst for the expression of all there is. The expression of all there is brings to you the essence of every living thing. The essence of every living thing lives in this energy. This life force and this power bring with it magic, magic, magic.

Magic brings the sense of power, light and "All Truth" is the magical ingredient, as it balances out the heart's emotional yearning to be loved by someone outside yourself.

Now try and imagine a world where you could live completely lovingly, abundantly and truthfully without the need for love outside yourself. There is no craving, no longing, just a simple knowing that love from this source is available and ready to enter and create with you all you need right now!

Just for one day try living without emotional craving for love, from the source outside yourself.

See, hear, taste, touch and smell right now with your heart's senses opened, your call to "All Truth" to bring you to this state of absoluteness in love.

Right now the embodiment of "All Truth" is a gift you can freely receive, because energy is not being directed to an object, outside yourself. Your freedom now becomes connected to source energy of "All Truth." Creating with this source energy is your complete acceptance of this magical power source.

For in feeling this magical power source you are opening up unbelievably to the world of power, power like an electrical transmitter energy source. For in this power is raw transformative energy, one of completeness for all there is. Allowing now the source power, the source energy to create with you, allows the forces of nature, the elements and their quarters to create with you in a new way. The essence of truth lives in the mystery. The essence of truth lives with all there is.

Feeling the expression of this force creates with it an almighty sense of raw atomic energy in your whole being. Imagine now source energy of "All Truth" at your disposal.

What are you going to do with it?

You are going to use it to transform consciousness and bring you into alignment with all there is. Feeling this energy and creating with it brings power, light and peace.

Feeling the power of "All Truth" to create with you now allows the absoluteness of all there ever was, and will be to create with you. Allowing this space to create with you allows even more light and power to be yours now. This sense of allowance brings with it truth and magic for the essence of who you are. The essence of who you are rides the wave when you create with the "All Truth" guides, because there is no going back.

There is no going back now when you create in this energy because you are allowing yourself the magic of all you ever were to create with you. This essence brings with it the pure simple pleasure, the pure simple peace to really feel the results of the energy. All energy downloads must produce results, and you must now be a witness to the results you are getting.

What are the results in my life so far, since I have been creating with the "All Truth" guides? What are the results now?

Stop now: Review your journey with the "All Truth" guides.

What has happened in your life? What has happened?

The essence of "All Truth" lives in an opened heart.

How has your heart opened? How has your heart created with you?

List as many things about your life that have changed since you began creating with the "All Truth" guides.

You must feel these effects flow into your heart and allow the energy of them to bring you to a space of pure power and light for all there is. This raw power has no parallel in any previous reality when you begin to consciously tap into it. There is a need to really surrender to this power and see the mind as a servant, a tool of the intelligent heart. Your mind now begins to ask directions. It obeys the intelligent heart flowing energy into the heart's power station to create cooperation, rather than domination.

You are flowing and creating in this energy now, driving power into yourself to heal and receive. The essence of this receiving has encoded in it a sense of absolute truth for all there is. You are resurrecting yourself at a time of the most incredible power and light show you can imagine, powering up your life now brings even more power and light to you. This is your power. This is your truth.

"All Truth" creates power. Your definition of power in your mind's framework has no parallel in any reality we are presenting you with. Your mind has what has been presented to it as power. (i.e. Power tools, powerful people, weapons, cars) They are usually a masculine definition of power. They create a masculine framework for this definition now. A truly powerful person cannot be defined by these external subjective expressions.

The Divine Feminine is the source of power for "All Truth," because it recognizes the principle of "self nurturing." Power comes from "self nurturing." Power comes from recognizing that "self nurturing" earths the power. Power through "All Truth" can only come from "self nurturing." The principle of "self nurturing" is behind all that is life affirming in your world.

You must seek now to really understand the principle of "self nurturing," to create change in the whole molecular structure of your cells.

The power of "All Truth" is the power to earth; to self-nurture and to receive.

This is power.

This is power for you now to really feel the enormous challenge in your humanness.

Feel this power now. Breathe it in, and above all, earth it.

Feeling "All Truth" through the heart activations begins now. Feeling truth brings more power. To feel truth is to be in the company of the almighty forces, which shape our destiny. To feel this energy brings power and births power to you. You are feeling the weight of all responsibilities lifted when you begin to create with "All Truth."

Creating with "All Truth" allows magic and life force to flow through you. It balances up your receiving through the masculine and it brings the masculine back into balance with the feminine. The force of the feminine is balanced with the masculine. The force of the feminine holds itself through the masculine.

When the "All Truth" vibration becomes enacted there is a shifting of energy in the body; an alignment takes place: *The force of "All Love," through The Feminine, (the Mt DNA, refer to my book Awaken your Immortal Intelligent Heart) can be further supported by The Masculine of "All Truth."*

You are exploring the sense of balance when you activate these forces. These forces are activated and energized; they bring power, strength and light.

Allow the forces of The Divine Masculine to balance the scales of The Divine Feminine; by creating "All Truth" as a counterpart to "All Love." Feeling this balance in your heart now helps your integration of energy selves.

Your own belief in "All Truth" brings to you the very nature of what truth is. The very nature of what truth is must be reflected on and absorbed into your central core matrix, for you to receive the precious gift of an "All Truthful" way of life.

You are vibrating to an "All Truth"-filled way of being human when you reflect on the magic of "All Truth," and what it will bring you right now. Bringing "All Truth" to you and birthing it in your cellular remembering is an act of love for yourself. This act of love for yourself reflects the preciousness of an "All Truth"-filled way of being human. Your "Truth" becomes an object for you to attain. Your "Truth" becomes your beacon.

Your ability to hold light for "All Truth" brings a truth-filled way of being human to you. Every single molecule has "All Truth" encoded in it when you receive the gift of "All Truth" for yourself. Just feel this preciousness now in your cellular remembering, bring to you now the world of absoluteness in everything. Absoluteness creates order, truth and dignity. You are vibrating to the world of absoluteness now. Feeling the gift of absoluteness brings to you "All Truth," power and light. You are now creating with this way of being now. It balances your ability to receive love.

Your journey now creates a sense of absoluteness and you are being recoded every single moment you say "yes" to receiving love; for receiving love embodies truth. Receiving love creates a truth-filled way of being human.

How can you receive love?

It is the consciousness, which is important. Right now, your consciousness is being coded to receive love. When your consciousness becomes encoded to receive love, love can be poured into your central core matrix, in the cellular remembering. You are allowing your precious sense of remembering to bring you back to what is rightfully yours as a human.

A human's right to love on this planet completely aware of why they are here is part of what you are creating with right now. The sense of this connection with your core remembering brings this precious sense of remembering to you. You are aware of the possibilities of being human and Divine all at once. There is a strength and commitment to being human and a true knowing why you are here and why you have taken life on this planet. Your gift to yourself is in this remembering now.

Beginning a new journey to freedom through the "All Truth" guides allows your heart to receive every moment. For you do not allow yourself to be compromised by people and events which cause circumstances to destabilize your truth.

You are alive to receiving when truth is encoded in your cellular remembering, as you do not allow situations to emerge, which create barriers to receiving. You are allowing a truth-filled way of being to encode you now.

This encodement has at its heart, peace. Simple peace, order and stillness. Peace, order and stillness create in you now a sense of absoluteness for everything. Everything is absolute in your life now, when you know your situations are truth filled for you. Just now you are birthing this reality, as a way of being human. Feeling this now brings to you peace, order and respect. Feeling peace, order and respect allows in you love, "self love."

Observe any situation in your life where you are being challenged and ask yourself:

Does it bring me peace, order and self-respect?

You only need to evoke for a connection to "All Truth" to create in you this sense of peace, order and self-respect. Feeling this now allows the sense of wonder to be encoded in you. This sense of wonder creates a knowing that every living thing supports your journey. You are at this stage of cellular remembering now.

Right now "All Truth" shapes the course of your destiny, because "All Truth" has encoded in it this sense of complete detachment from the past. Detachment from the past brings power, unbelievable raw power, which must be channelled into a sense of new beginning for all there is.

Who are we as humans, if we cannot have this sense of truth and justice encoded in us? This truth and justice brings with it a sense of raw power which can give you, the seeker of truth, a sense of such detachment and light, it takes away all fear of being listened to. It takes away all fear of not getting a "fair hearing." The "Truth" of the Ancient Egyptian religious and social system was "Maat's" law, as a system of justice, which was pure and uncontaminated. You are witnessing this unbelievable sense of "Maat's" power now.

You are beginning to really feel the power of "Maat" as a system and way of being. The feeling brings unimaginable joy, peace and light. Joy, peace and light create with you to really allow you — the seeker of truth, power and respect — to bring you all you need for a life of perfect balance and harmony. Feeling this now brings light, peace and order, you are "Maat" now.

"Maat" is the Goddess of "All Truth." Right now you are embodying the system, the ancient universal system of law, order and justice. This system brings with it the truth and magic of all of life creating with you now. You are listening to only one thing, and this is the law of truth for the soul.

The law of truth for the soul brings to you the source of "All Love." The source of "All Love" is revealed to you now, as you begin the journey to reclaim your own power through truth. The power to reclaim your source remembering through truth awakens you now to the power of the mystery. You are revealing to yourself now this source of power and light.

The source of power and light brings to you all you ever were, and all you ever will become. Just allowing this power and light to resurrect you brings you to the essence of your core remembering. The essence of your core remembering brings to you now, weapons, weapons to truly fight for your heart's intelligence. The heart's remembering, its essence of remembering creates with you, the perfect challenge to create in the essence of "now."

The essence of "now" is in this remembering all you ever were and all you will ever become. For it's all in this power, this remembering, this truth. The essence of remembering lives in your immortal heart.

Feeling the flow of this remembering brings with it a sense of absoluteness for the mystery. For absoluteness in the mystery allows sweet remembering to surface. Allowing sweet remembering to surface brings you all you ever need in the human journey. You are alive to this remembering now, as the forces of all there ever was brings you home to you.

You are magical in this essence and a force of almighty power. Humans must consciously want this power, light, peace and order and continually strive to create with it. You are flowing in this essence, this remembering now. You are allowing these happenings to create with you in the mystery. The mystery is just that; your story. You want the complete picture of your life in this story, and you want to feel this magical essence in all of life.

The essence of all life brings with it a sense of the mystery. The mystery brings power, peace and light. Creating with power, peace and light enfolds you now, as you allow your own heart to shine; your shining heart now gleams because it is radiating power, peace, light and order. Allowing this essence to create with you brings all you ever were to you. You are "All Love" and "All Truth" now.

Creating with the "All Truth" guides allows power through the masculine to be manifested. You are witnessing this power now. The "All Truth" guides are creating in a powerful way, your new reality. This reality has encoded in it "All." "All" means the "All" of everything.

You want "All Truth" when you know there cannot be true justice in the world of the unbalanced masculine. The masculine principle of protection, order and truth, cannot be properly enacted in your world. Your world is one of enacting truth and living truthfully.

Living truthfully brings power, light and a complete understanding of what it is to be human. Your power and light becomes an experience for you to witness daily. You are creating a vortex of raw power and light now. This sense of raw power and light magnetizes to you, all you ever were; all you ever were brings truth to the process of allowing. Allowing power to be manifested through "All Truth" creates a vortex of raw magical power, anchoring your heart and giving it more nourishment to stay in the body. Bringing in this sense of truth brings to you now, the power, light and magic of all you ever were. All you ever were is truth made manifest.

Trust is the principle behind "All Truth." "All Truth" requires trust in the principle of order to be enacted. Trust in something; whether it is a relationship, project or belief, is something that is encoded in you.

"I trust the principle of 'All Truth' to guide this work; this endeavour; this belief."

When you bring trust into the vibration of "All Truth" you are creating a worldview that makes you go beyond your previously held definition of what trust is. You are enacting the mystery, and raw power is being made available to you. As a human, you go beyond your definition of what it is to be human.

You trust the principle of "All Truth" to give you what you asked for. This is your belief in the principle of law, order and light over fear, darkness and despair. Despair is a total breakdown of the heart's intelligence to create with you. The heart's intelligence can only flower when it knows it is protected by the principle of "All Truth" to manifest the new creation.

The "Black Heart" of pure dissolution; the point of singularity; the Goddess void must begin the creation again after its regeneration. Regeneration creates peace, space and order to begin the journey to the next level of consciousness. This next level of consciousness will be enacted with the consciousness of "All Truth."

You are delivering to your heart the belief that it can regenerate and rejuvenate, through the masculine principle of "All Truth."

Allowing now your perfect self to emerge with the "All Truth" guides brings a level of support for your whole being. Your own essence has been made whole, and you can really see why you have created a space within yourself for this to be happening right now.

Your world brings to you this complete acceptance of yourself in every way. Your truth is a beacon of powerful light, now ready to guide and shape your beingness. Your beingness has encoded in it now a powerful weapon of truth.

Truth is the master intelligence guiding the forces of creation. In the moment of creation, truth becomes enacted. There is a sense of power, majesty and might with the "All Truth" guides. Power, majesty and might bring to you the forces of remembering. Remembering to be part of these almighty forces shapes your reality.

Why are you here? You are here on earth to experience these forces while in a body, living with your own emotional chaos most of the time, dealing with the mind, which can destroy in an instant if not guarded.

These are you enemies in being human; your emotional body and your mind body. Weapons must be used against them, when they become chaotic. *The weapons of "All Truth" are evoked. Remember to reinforce to the mind and emotions.*

"Is this 'situation' truth filled to my fully awakened intelligent heart?"

We are here to protect the heart, the "All Love" centre, the power generator. "Truth" protects the heart.

The "All Truth" guides allow you now to really create a world, which offers simple peace. This peace can be enacted anytime. This peace is instant and can be activated, like switching on a light. You are allowing this peace to become part of your cellular matrix. This peace brings simple order and light.

This peace brings to your world a sense of absoluteness in the process of being human. Your peace-filled heart is filled with light when you evoke the "All Truth" guides. *Why?* When a heart is peace-filled, "All Truth" can be enacted. "All Truth" brings to you simple power and light; truth becomes enacted and you become a beacon of incredible light and power. Seeing this power, hearing it, tasting it, smelling it and touching it, brings incredible light to your aura, energy field and light body. Your humanness is your own power station, and you can really create with it. Creating with humanness through "All Truth" brings power, light and incredible strength.

Why should we not have these gifts as humans? It's like knowing you can have a car with all the power you need and choosing to ride a bike! Enjoy the ride!

You have felt the new energy of "All Truth" truly work for you. You are alive to the power and light of "All Truth." You are observing total detachment to everything that is not connected to you. You are seeing your energy is important and not wasting it on anyone. "You" are important and so is your heart.

You are observing "receiving" in action. You are receiving every moment you enact truth. When you enact truth by saying: "'All Truth' be with me now," you are in actual fact receiving. This is opening the heart (self centre) even farther. Keep your "All Truth" centre opened continuously, this feeds energy to the heart (self centre).

You are witnessing now the emergence of "All Truth" as an energetic force, which brings to you the power and light of your surrender. You are witnessing all aspects of your total self create with the heart for all there is. The heart of all there is; is you. Just you.

You are the heart of "All" there is.

This essence has encoded in it power, power, power. Power brings the force of it "All" with you. Power brings the essence of every living thing to you. Power is your greatest weapon against evil. Power, power, power; always evoke "All Truth."

The essence of "All Truth" lies in the force of remembering. The force of remembering is in enacting ritual, order and light. Ritual, order and light bring more order, ritual and light to you. Feeling this essence brings light, peace and order. There is an almighty force awaiting you now, the almighty force is the essence of your truth and power. The essence of your truth and power creates with you in the mystery.

Feeling this mystery creates power. Feeling this mystery creates order. Feeling this mystery creates in you now the simple joy of knowing you are safe in your world and this world is perfect for you right now.

This simple truth is that your world is perfectly safe even in chaos, especially in chaos. Chaos is the opportunity to re-create order. Chaos brings order. Celebrate chaos, really celebrate chaos, as you step into it, you are demanding order immediately.

If you have an emergency such as a fire is burning your home (chaos); you create order by demanding the force of chaos (the fire), be under the Divine will of "All Truth." The force of chaos has no chance now, because the fire brigade has been called. Chaos has been contained.

The "All Truth" guides allow you now the spirit of trust between yourself and them to emerge. The spirit of trust is a deepening love and a knowing that they are "beings" you can trust to call on to bring forth the source of light and power for all there is. The true spirit of trust merges in oneness with you now and this spirit of trust must be fostered and developed.

Allowing this trust to create with you, allows the spirit of truth to be enacted in you at a deeper and purer level. This energy has at its heart the essence, energy and life force of all there is. The essence, energy and life force brings with it a sense of truth and power for the mystery. The mystery is enacted in this supreme vibration.

You are allowing yourself to merge in this gathering now deeper, deeper and deeper into the heart of the mysteries. The mysteries have at their heart this deepening of your love for this truth. The essence of love is to have a deepening of love and power for the mystery of it all. The mystery of your power is in the enactment of truth and "All Truth" holds the power.

We are alchemizing the process of forgiveness for the human condition. The human condition is a forgiveness process. Every single human on the planet must forgive himself or herself every day for one aspect of "being human." Every single aspect of "being human" is a forgiveness of the past. The essence of the past is a forgiveness process. Forgive yourself to the trespass of yourself to yourself right now. This forgiveness has encoded in it the process of absolute alchemy. This alchemical process brings with it a sense of real truth for the mystery.

Real truth for the mystery brings this forgiveness process into alignment with the forces of absoluteness. The forces of absoluteness are about the purity of humanity's ability to love the truth. To love the truth is one of the most sacred acts a human is capable of reaching. It is the target to the "Black Heart" of forgiveness and dissolution. The "Black Heart" of dissolution is the "Black Heart" of Bliss.

The "Black Heart" of Bliss is the force of mergence, then dissolution and re-mergence, forming and aligning the forces of truth to re-create again. The forces of truth create with you. The forces of truth merge, dissolve, re-create and embody the alchemy of "All there is".

The alchemy of "All there is," allows the sacred essence of the mysteries to become one with the essence, energy and life force of truth for the mystery. This is "truth."

Trusting in the all-truth process brings to you the sense of absolute truth in everything. Truth has its own power, and power brings truth into alignment with all there is. "All there is" is a truth-filled experience. Your life is a truth-filled magical experience, your essence vibrates to this source, and this source has at its heart, a space of truth and love for the mystery.

Allowing the heart of truth to create with you brings a sense of absoluteness for every living thing. This vibration creates wonder, energy and life force. Wonder, energy and life force are the essence of the mystery. You are allowing this energy to bring you to the absoluteness of all there ever was.

Feeling the absoluteness of truth brings with it even more power and light. Light and power feed truth, and a truth-filled loving experience; your experience of loving truth, and walking on the direct path of truth, brings with it the greatest power. Raw magical transformative power brings to you the heart of yourself in the alchemical tradition. You are allowing truth to be the master. Truth creates the master. Truth is the master.

The force of truth cannot be underestimated, for it has contained in it power, power and more power. The essence of truth lives with the mystery of creation; you are vibrating to the pure matter of truth being an alchemical process. Truth is an alchemical process.

You are experiencing now the essence of what it is to be powerful. The essence of what it is to be powerful is truth. Truth makes power create with you. Truth is the magical weapon of power. You are feeling the magical alchemy of power create with you now, as you open your heart to the mystery. You are feeling this essence, this magical power in your whole being as you bring to your world the essence, energy and life force of power.

The essence, energy and life force bring magical intent. Magical intent brings power and light. Flowing with this energy allows the power of all you ever were to bring you the essence, energy and life force right now.

You are feeling now power drive your abundance.

"My abundance is my power. My abundant heart is my power."

You are magnetizing to you now the power of an abundant heart that brings power and a mighty force to you now.

You are creating in this power now, and you are creating a world of absoluteness in everything. Allowing you now this power, peace and light to envelope you brings you into resonance with all there is. You are feeling this power now. Your weapons are in creating a model for power, light and beauty. Celebrate, and magnetize this power to you now.

"All Truth" brings focus, clarity and direction. "All Truth" brings a sense of respect for all life, and all living things including their consciousness, as it is their journey. You must allow this magical journey to gather momentum now, and you must feel the essence of this magic gather force and power.

The essence of force is the alchemizing of events, circumstances, nature and the natural world to envelope you. *Why?* Because your consciousness does not match the collective consciousness. You are allowing the force of magical intent to magnetize the force of the natural world to create with you.

You are just flowing now with the force of power and light to magnetize all the magician requires. This magnetic energy brings with it a sense, a true sense of pure purpose and light. True purpose and light bring order and magical energy. You are encoding yourself for this now.

"All Truth" now begins to manifest for you, as you create a vortex of power in "love." You are allowing this sense of power and light to create as "All Love" has a companion—"All Truth." You are witnessing the power, essence and light of "All Love and All Truth" to bring you to the epic-centre of "All." All magical love has at its heart this centre. This point of singularity, this point of no return; where all is one and one is all.

You are allowing right now the sense of absoluteness to be your mentor and guide and absoluteness is the only creation. Absoluteness is the only creation there is. The creation of absoluteness is in "absoluting" yourself from your pain in love in being human.

Humanness imposes on you, your greatest challenge, and the challenge is to see emotional love as a by-product. A by-product (like a waste product) of the power of alchemy through love. You cannot truly manifest a self-sustainable reality in your world, without committing to examining the reality of love as a self-sustainable reality. This reality has at its core "self." The "self" is you. It is not a by-product. It is not a waste product.

A self-sustaining reality brings you into resonance with your truth, power and light. Receive this gift now. The challenge to create a world of magical love brings you the gift of your fully awakened intelligent heart. Sustain your reality; go to the heart for answers.

You are now allowing the source energy of your magical life to create with you all you need to love. For love renews itself in the bath of mystery. Allowing the experience of "All Truth" to be the alchemizing agent to bring light, energy and source power to you. Light, energy and source power provide truth for the mystery of being human.

Being human is a truth-filled experience. Truth is the greatest elixir you can give your heart right now, as you channel the power of your fully awakened intelligent heart. The heart of "All Truth" has the most powerful charge. It is an electrical current, ready to create with you. Your energy just propels into a skyward rocket exploding and creating even more power and light. For the mystery of who you are. You are an immortal woman. All creation comes from the space of immortality.

You are alive to this creation now. Dive deep into the well of immortality where there is no pain, no fear and no anxiety. Imagine now, diving deep into the well of nothing that is only pure, light and magic. Feeling this magical flow brings you to the heart of all there is. You are love; truly just love in the mystery of "All Truth." Feeling this now brings power, light and truth. "All Love and All Truth" are alchemizing now.

You are receiving power through the mystery. This power has at its source, the energy and light of your own magical self. The essence and light of your magical self grows in the mystery. Right now you must create in this mystery. You must create in the mystery of who you are and you must feel the power of the mystery surround you.

Believing in your ability to receive in the mystery reinforces all you ever were and all you ever will be. There is a force and magic in this energy, and you must feel this power and magic merge with you in oneness for all there is.

Allowing yourself to trust in magic brings you to the point of no return. The point of no return creates in the essence of this remembering who you ever were: You are one in essence with this force now. May the force of all you ever were in "All Truth" guide you now. You are "All Truth."

Your energy must now flow to the heart of truth and attach to the heart of truth. The heart of truth creates with you now. Allowing the heart of truth to bring you your power, essence and life force, reinforces in you now, the gift of knowing your heart and the heart of "All Truth" are one.

You are the heart of "All Truth" and the heart of "All Truth" is being made available to you now. You are being consecrated and energized into the heart of "All Truth" now. The heart of "All Truth" nourishes you and supports you now.

You are now open to the heart of "All Truth," feel and experience the heart of "All Truth" giving you all you need to nourish your inner power.

The "All Truth" guides are a mighty force. Bring them in and manifest with them now. They are manifestable beings. Heart of "All Truth": I Love You.

"All Truth" is truly manifestable, because "All Truth" provides energy and clarity. Energy and clarity are needed to create a world which recognizes you are the sole centre of your creation and you create the shift for this creation to manifest.

You are allowing the essence of manifestation to create with you now, as you bring to your world peace and light. The energy of light is such an important resource, and the energy of light brings you to a point of balance and order for all there is.

You are allowing this sense of power and light to become one with you now. You are focusing now on allowing the essence of your absoluteness to bring you to the heart of truth. The heart of "All Truth" creates in wonder for all there is.

It is time to allow the spirit of allowance of all there is to bring your heart to you; and when the heart is charged with the vibration of "All Truth" it becomes the greatest weapon you can fight with. Feeling the heart of truth brings power, magic and light. You are allowing this energy to create with you now.

Your frequency to hold the vibration of "All Truth" is growing, and you must allow your heart to be strengthened by the "All Truth" vibration. Right now "All Truth" brings peace, space and order to the heart, for the heart is in constant peril.

Why am I here?

It is urgent right now to really look at "Why am I here?"

Well, *"Why am I here?"*

At a time of enormous upheaval on our earth, this is the most opportune time to test your old reality against the new energy. Allow this energy to bring you to the heart of truth. The heart of truth has at its core the relationship with all living things existing in harmony with each other.

These energies are available now. These energies are making us aware of our power to create a world that offers truth and light.

Truth and light bring power, and your power is in drawing on truth and light.

Feel this now in your molecular structure. Feel the power of knowing "you" are bringing to your world, this strength and light.

This strength and light creates magic; your world becomes a magical experience. You are alive to this now. You become an electrical magical being with the energy of "All Truth." Flow with this magic now. Flow with it.

The "All Truth" guides create a sense of absoluteness in everything. The sense of absoluteness brings Bliss.

The sense of allowing "All Truth" to be part of your own cellular memory creates a space for Bliss to envelope you.

"All Truth" manifests a new reality. Manifesting a new reality allows a sense of absoluteness to become one with your own cellular remembering. Right now, cellular remembering brings with it a sense of truth for the mystery. The mystery of who you are and the mystery of your magical power become magnified with "All Truth."

"All Truth" creates a vortex of raw magical power, which creates through the essence of "All Truth."

You are alive to the meaning of what being truth filled really is. You are alive to the essence of truth.

You are allowing "you," and your "youth" magnifies and intensifies with youth. Youth is you. Children are themselves. You. Me. It's me because their critical minds haven't developed to challenge the youth-filled heart.

So it is with anyone who is truth filled. There is a simple joy in living. Why carry lies and deceit?

Why carry untruths?

You are alive to the essence of truth. You are alive to the essence of allowing "you."

"You" the power of "you."

"You" and "you" are one. One is the essence of "you."

"You" only, brings youth, power and light.

"All Truth" brings now a sense of separation from your old identity. Who you were, is not who you are now. Who you were is in the past. Who you are now is the present. *Trust this present; trust in the process of now; trust in the spirit of all you are now.*

This trust, this presence, brings peace, space, order, abundance and, above all, the ability to receive love. The ability to receive love is the greatest gift you can give yourself; because you are the object, you are the object of all you ever were and will be, just you, just your ability to receive love.

Love is you. Love is real. Love is the joy of saying:

"I can love."

"I am love."

"I trust love."

"All Truth" brings "All Love" to you in a way you cannot possibly imagine. "All Truth" creates meaning to life. "All Truth" creates a vortex of power. Power, light and truth are yours now.

"All Truth" creates meaning in life; life is one of surrender. Every act of growth must have surrender encoded in it. Surrender implies power, light and truth and a knowing that you are resilient and can create a world of magnificent power to bring your world its truth.

To deliver truth is a mighty responsibility. It creates with it great power and absolute trust in the essence of all you ever were. Bringing this truth into resonance with your core identity shapes and creates. Shaping and creating "you" brings an unbelievable level of light and power.

Light and power give you strength, and an almighty belief in all you ever were. All you ever were confers upon you power and truth.

You are alive to the essence of all there ever was, and you are alive to the possibilities now of knowing you and "All Truth" create a vortex of raw magical power.

Feeling and sensing this energy and light allows truth to become encoded in your cellular matrix. The world of "Truth" envelops you. You become one with the mystery.

You are now vibrating to "All Truth."

This is a powerful time for you, because you are releasing your previously held belief about yourself, and going to a world of light, power and energy. You are one in essence with all of life, and all of life respects your need now to create a space of forgiveness for everything in your life.

You are now allowing this space to envelope you and keep you in a space of absoluteness for everything in your life. When you are powerful, you are truthful. Power and truth bring respect for every living thing. The sense of power brings to you order. Order confers discipline in everything. Everything ordered is disciplined.

Bringing this peace and order brings light. Light doesn't dissipate. Light creates a vortex of power when it can be beamed strongly on an object.

Feel this now.

Light. Power. Order. Discipline.

These are the hallmarks of a disciplined person.

"All Truth" brings to you now a sense of complete understanding for the workings of yourself in your universe. "All Truth" allows a sense of absoluteness for the mystery. The sense of absoluteness for the mystery brings a sense of real forgiveness and light for all there is.

Right now you are shining in the energies of "All Truth." "All Truth" brings stability and order for you in the absoluteness of who you are. Radiating absoluteness brings power. Radiating absoluteness brings a sense of order. You are allowing this sense of true power and absoluteness to guide you. True power and absoluteness brings light, peace and order.

This power comes from the sense of absoluteness. Your absoluteness brings you into alignment with all the forces of truth for the mystery. Allow now the spirit of trust to bring you into resonance with all there is.

You are a light being radiating power, energy and light. Shine!

Bringing "All Truth" into alignment with your beingness creates in you a sense of magic and order. There is a sense of true magic and order in everything. Everything has this encodement in it. Encodement brings you now a sense of respect for every living thing. This sense of respect for every living thing has power and light encoded in it. Truth, light and power are yours now. You are vibrating to this way of being human. Humanness is order manifested. All manifestable order and truth brings magic and the essence of every living thing. You are radiating to this sense of magical essence now.

"All Truth" brings now a sense of true ownership of all creations. The ownership of all creations brings the mystery into alignment with who "you" are. You are feeling now the true sense of power and light bring you all you need to love. You need to really just allow the sense of magic and light to bring you all you need to create a world with only you in it. Allow yourself now to find a space where "you" get the totality of who "you" are and allow that totality to really create with you. You cannot create anything unless the totality; the sum totality of who you are is included. The essence of your shining self is to be shined on you. You are the shining one. This is an exacting and important time for you. Allow your essence to shine.

Embodying The Divine Masculine of All Truth, Through The High Priest

"I now love my truth-filled heart."
"I now love my truth-filled heart."
"Truth-filled heart, I love you."

"All Truth" shapes your reality. The essence of it truly shapes your totality, and brings it into alignment with all there is. "All Truth" brings to your world, this essence and this energy. The energy and essence of your totality is in the world of "All Truth."

"All Truth" allows "you" your heart; your belief in your truth to shine. This is an important time to really see and experience "All Truth" for what it is. It is a friend. See "All Truth" as a very wise and trusted friend. Wise and trusted friends create a grid of special protection around all parts of your "self" that really need to feel. This sense of feeling has at its core power, truth and light.

You are feeling power to really pour light to the emotionally fragmented aspect of your "self." Right now, you are needing to Earth this power and feel that this new part of your "self" brings with it a sense of totality for your troubled "selves"; your emotional "self."

Getting your emotional "self" under the handle of your "All Truth" self brings power, light and order. Your "All Truth" self is your wise friend.

You are magnifying truth when you consider you are bringing to your world a sense of absoluteness in everything. Everything has absoluteness encoded in it. This expansion brings with it peace, space and order.

This peace, space and order allow for more energy and light to gather in your whole being. Getting peace, space and order brings light and a complete sense of knowing that at "The Heart" of you, the real Heart; "The Black Heart" is a sense of absoluteness in everything.

Everything is absolute in your world. Right now, you must energize yourself and engage yourself in allowing the true sense of all you ever were to bring "you" peace and light.

Feeling this peace and light brings truth and power; truth and power to allow you a sense of oneness with mystery. Feeling now the essence of your own power brings even more power to you. You are vibrating now to the sense of power and light. This sense of power and light brings with it a sense of absoluteness. *Absoluteness has encoded in it – love. All absoluteness is "Love."*

Love is absoluteness manifested.

You are allowing love as a manifestable reality to be yours now. You are allowing this manifestable reality to shape you. When you create with the intent of drawing down "All Truth" as a way of being, you are manifesting "Truth." You are manifesting love and you are manifesting a belief in your totality.

This energy has at its core — power.
Powerful people manifest truth.
Powerful people manifest love.
You are alive to the possibilities of manifesting love through truth.

Allowing this manifestation to be earthed is essential right now. You are one in essence with manifestable power because "All Truth" brings this power to you.

"All Truth" brings peace. Evoking "All Truth" creates in the heart a sense of balance especially when it is awakening. It is important to create in this cycle, not destroy. Destruction creates fear; fear must be given no energy. Laugh at fear. Give it no energy. "All Truth" is a membrane that encloses fear and dissolves fear. You are remembering that fear creates a barrier to integration. Fear creates distrust in remembering. Fear is greedy, nasty and envious. It has all the attributes of evil. And it must not be given any energy.

"All Love" is like a shoot of green grass, growing in a jungle of fear. *"All Truth" protects "All Love" to grow.* "All Truth" brings "All Love" hope to keep growing in the jungle of weeds. The weeds choke. Now fear is given no energy. "All Truth" prevents fear from choking "All Love."

All day, every day, ask for "All Truth" to protect your creations.

All this affirmation to percolate your consciousness so "All Truth" can be embodied against "all fear":

"All my creations are now protected by 'All Truth.'"

Finding now your power to create with the essence of all there is brings you to the absolute heart of all you ever were. This essence of all you ever were is the "All Truth"-filled aspect of yourself. This aspect brings with it the essence of "All Light, Truth and Power."

Power, truth and light bring with it the magic of renewal and resurrection. Staying in the portal of remembering, allows this essence of your truth to be embodied by you. Your truth is an embodiment of all there ever was.

Your truth reflects the embodiment of your sacred essence self. Your sacred essence self brings with it this truth. Truth is measured by your power to really love the part of yourself that knows no fear. Embracing the shadow, embracing the fear, brings you to the space within yourself that knows only one thing, your truth-filled heart.

"All Truth" allows the forces to create with you in magic. "All Truth" brings down the alchemical tradition in its purest and most realizable form. "All Truth" just carves out a space of absoluteness for all there is. Absoluteness for all there is allows the forces of magic to envelope you. The power of surrendering to the magic, the power to create with the magical tradition brings you to raw source power. Light, energy and power are now yours. The source energy of this light, energy and power bring with it raw transformative energy. Raw transformative energy brings you to a sense of truth for all there is. The source magical energy brings with it power, truth and light.

Power, truth and light create the vortex of raw magical power for your own hearts truth to manifest. Feeling this now brings to you the essence of "All Truth." The essence of "All Truth" is the alchemizing force behind the mystery. The mystery of "All Truth" is in the knowledge that you are able to really create a space of real energy; light and power in all "you" are capable of. You are the essence of this alchemizing force now.

"All Truth" allows the magic of renewal to create with you. You are under the essence energy and life force of "All Truth" in everything. Every living thing has "All Truth" encoded in it. "All Truth" is the sum total of every living thing. "All Truth" witnesses the emergence of your absoluteness in everything. This absoluteness creates a space of pure light for the mystery. The mystery of who "you" are is an alchemizing force. This alchemizing force brings power; raw, magical power. This raw, magical power has at its core the truth of the mystery. The mystery holds and encodes truth in it. This truth liberates you from enslavement. Enslavement creates separation. Separation from your truth creates chaos.

"All Truth" provides a framework for the source energy of "All Love." *"All Love's" source energy comes through "All Truth."* Feeling "All Truth" brings the special mystery alive in your heart. The mystery of being alive in your heart allows peace and light to be your guide. You are vibrating to this sense of peace and light now. This is a time to feel the magnification of peace and light in your energetic matrix. Peace and light bring power, respect and order. You are vibrating to this sense of peace, space and order now in your cellular remembering. Feeling this energy brings light. Pure light concentrated into every cell and membrane, releasing old core fears and patterns.

You are free now to develop your relationship with "All Truth" as a way of being human. This truth brings with it completeness. When you are truthful you are complete. The essence of completeness lives in the energy of you and your total relationship with all there is. Allowing this flow, this magic, brings you to the core essence of all you ever were.

Embodying The Divine Masculine of All Truth, Through The High Priest

Your allowance of "All Truth" brings light and power. Light and power allow the mystery to unfold. Allowing the mystery to unfold creates a vortex of power and truth for all there is.

You must allow this flow to bring you all you need to love the part of yourself that is disconnected. Plug into this reality now. Really plug into the core remembering of all you ever were now. Allowance of this special magic brings joy and light. You are "All Truth" now.

Bringing through the power of all you ever were, allows the mystery to really create with you. This mystery is at the heart of all there ever was. The mystery of your enfoldment is a gift of allowing the essence; energy and life force bring you all you need to experience the world of absoluteness in everything. The essence and love of your new world brings with it all you ever were. All you ever were allows the magical intent of your magnificent life to create with you. This magnificent life has truth encoded in it.

Truth now is encoded in everything. The encodement of truth in everything brings to you power and light. You can open up now to the world of truth in everything.

Allowing now the power of the mystery brings to you the essence of all there ever was to you. You are vibrating to the mystery of yourself. You are the greatest mystery, your essence is the mystery, and it is creation itself. The essence of creation brings you to the seat of your power.

The essence of all you ever were is encoded in "All Truth." Your magical essence brings with it magic and peace. It is time to really feel this nourishment and peace. Allowing this now brings more to you. You are allowing this to bring you home to the creative essence of yourself. The feeling of creative essence in enacting ritual through "All Truth" brings you to the core essence of all you ever were.

Allowing this power, this magical essence and power, brings to you now the ability to really connect to your own belief in the magic of all you ever were. You are alive to this essence, this magic now. Feeling the flow, the energetic flow, allows you now the power, the might and the magic of your immortal heart right now to fuse with the alchemical process in merging with "All Truth." Flow now with the essence, the energy and the life force of all you ever were. You are one in this essence now.

"All Truth" nourishes your core being because there is no struggle. The struggle is gone. Imagine life without "the struggle!" The essence of your being shines. The true essence of all you are brings you all you need to feel, see, touch, taste and hear, the power of "All Truth" to heal you. You are opening up yourself to this view of your reality right now. This view of your reality has at its core the self-nourishment a human needs to create a magical world.

This magical world is the energy of all you ever were and will be. All of your life propels you to this view of your reality right now. "All Truth" brings nourishment to your core being because there is no struggle.

"All Truth" enacts mystery. Mystery is enacted with "All Truth." "All Truth" brings power to enact mystery. When mystery is enacted, power comes. All power and light comes to you now. Truly allowing this power and light brings to you now the force of your remembering. The force of your remembering brings light and power. Allowing this force, this alchemizing force to create with you brings more energy, power and light to you. Allowing the energy of alchemy to create with you, allows you now the essence of your remembering.

Feeling the flow of the energy allows the magic of the energy to bring you more power and light. You are vibrating to this view of your reality now creating and alchemizing the forces. The forces are power; the forces are truth. Grow in the force, the alchemizing force of this truth and light now.

You need now to create with the flow of "All Truth" as a truly alchemizing force. You are allowing this alchemizing force to create with you in all areas of your life. Earth the alchemizing forces as you begin to really create a world view of pure trust for the mystery of alchemy right now. Trust in these forces; these forces require trust. Trusting in the forces brings the energy of the forces to you. This is a time to throw yourself into purely trusting the forces that serve you. The forces serve the mystery, and the mystery is to trust the forces.

Trusting "All Truth" to create with you is an ability to find within yourself the absolute essence of yourself creating with you all the time. You are creating now with the substance and absoluteness of "the force" behind "All Truth." "The Force" behind "All Truth" brings "All Truth" into your radar. The forces that shape all are the forces of "All Truth."

Flowing with this immutable force now leads your being in the presence of every living thing that shapes these forces. Allowing these forces shape to you brings you closer to the essence of every living thing. Every living thing has this force, this power, this remembering encoded in it.

These forces create with you and magnify your intent to consciously use the force for your new world. Create with these forces, and become them. You are love now.

You are now being brought closer to who you really are. The essence of any living thing lives in that perfect moment; that magical mystical moment when all is one, and one is all. You are allowing this mergence to bring you closer and closer to the part of yourself that creates in this essence now. You are witnessing now the dissolution of any previously held identity as you re-create all. All you are is what you can create with in that moment. In this moment, I am all I ever was and will become.

This is my epiphany; this is what I must leave behind, and I must now allow this old view of myself to go and re-create itself anew.

You are one in essence with this totality now. Allow yourself to receive in this "All Truth" way of being. You are the essence of it all.

Right now you are allowing the essence of this new identity to bring you peace and order. Truth becomes enacted with peace and order. Instability at every level sees no peace and order. When there is no peace and order you are open to negativity and fear. Truth in any form cannot stay in this space. This space brings fear and loss. Right now you are unlocking your own power to create a world of peace and order in your life. Just create in the essence of now. Just create in the essence of all there is. You are allowing this energy through "All Truth" to stamp itself upon you now.

The essence of truth lives in this expressive essence of all there is and will be. Allowing this expressive energy brings peace and light. You are witnessing now peace and light bring you all you need to create a world of absoluteness in everything.
"Just create in the essence of all there is."

The "All Truth" guides bring to you respect for the process of being human. The energy of respect for being human brings peace, space and order in your life. Allow this sense of peace, space and respect to bring you all you ever were. All you ever were brings power, light and energy. Power, light and energy bring to you all you ever were and will be.

Respect for the process of humanness brings to you now joy and peace. Peace, joy and light create in the mystery. The mystery is in the essence, the sum total of all you ever were. Allowing this essence brings the mystery to you. You are allowing now this energy to re-create itself in you as you bring to your world magic, light and truth. Right now, begin to use the "All Truth" guides in everything you do, and draw on the power and light they bring.

"All Truth" allows the spirit of truth to manifest for you. Truth is the greatest weapon to wield against evil. Evil cannot survive where there is truth. Truth is the most incredible energy, the most incredible power imaginable. You are resurrecting your power with "All Truth," because power, true power cannot come through without "All Truth." You are witnessing this power, this light and this truth now. All is one in the essence of truth. You are alive to the essence of truth and it brings to you all you ever were. Feeling, seeing, tasting, smelling and hearing "All Truth" is the greatest protective prayer/affirmation you can create with right now:

"This energy brings with it "All" you ever were. "All" you ever were is in allowance of 'All.' 'All Truth' is the sum total of "All" experiences."

Create with "All Truth" and you have the greatest weapon against evil.

"All Truth" creates a sense of absolute power because "All Truth" clears away all emotional debris. You are just sweeping away all emotional debris with "All Truth." This is a time to really feel the energy of "All Truth" manifesting for you. You are witnessing "All Truth" bring power, strength and light. Power, strength and light create through the mystery. The mystery of enactment is in "All Truth." Allowing the mystery of enactment brings "All Truth" to you now. You are one in essence with "All Truth." "All Truth" brings power, light and peace.

Right now there is a need to really create a sense of absoluteness with "All Truth." "All Truth" is an absolute expression of every living thing in the universe and beyond. You are shifting consciousness with "All Truth." Shifting consciousness implies that you, the "All Truth"-seeker and shaper, bring to your world this absoluteness in everything. Your sense of absoluteness allows you now to bring to your world this essence, this sense of magic and light for all you are. This essence and light brings to you now a weapon of absoluteness in everything.

"All Truth" creates a world view that supports all life. All life is supported and affirmed by "All Truth." "All Truth" brings to you now a respect for all living things. Every living thing has a right to live in a truth-filled way. Every living thing imagines itself being able to create in this balance at every moment. You are absoluting in this energy now. This sense of absoluting brings to you the sense of raw and powerful courage to make what you need in your life work for you. Now you are ready to really bring to this life "All" of everything. The "All" of everything has the "All" encoded in it.

"All Truth" creates a space of allowance for the true spirit of who "you" are manifest for you. Your life is a manifestable experience. All manifestable experiences create and come from "All Truth," and when completed give to "All Truth." You must continually reinforce now your commitment to "All Truth" as a way of being human.

"I can only be guided by 'All Truth.'"
"I am a witness to 'All Truth' manifesting for me and creating with me when I am truth filled for who I am."

Being truth filled for who "you" are allows magic to create with you.

"All Truth" allows you now to feel a sense of pure detachment in all you witness. You merely have to turn on the "All Truth" light for you to really allow the sense of absoluteness to encode itself on you. You must allow this sense of your own power now to ignite your consciousness and really feel what it is "you" need for your life of absoluteness in everything. You are allowing your own heart to say to you:
"I am free to pursue my own absoluteness in everything."

"Everything is absolute in my world."

You are allowing your own sense of truth to become "one" with "you." Your truth and you are one.

All you need to ask is:

"Is this serving 'All Truth'?"

"All Truth" creates now an amazing vortex of pure magical power, because energy bodies line up and become integrated, bringing the immortal heart into resonance with "All Love" and "All Truth." This is time to really feel "All Truth" as a manifestable thing, one that creates peace, space and order in your life. You are releasing all energies that do not serve you now as you create with the fire and heart of "Sekhmet". (The ancient Egyptian Goddess of power.) Your heart and fire brings raw magical power to "All Truth" as a way of being human. Flowing with this energy brings magic to you right now.

"All Truth" is a manifestable energy.

Right now the power of "All Truth" will create a vortex of invincibility in you. You become invincible to others and their demands on you. You become invincible to your own fears and limitations around your world right now. You are an invincible being right now. To become invincible brings to you a sense of absoluteness in everything. Everything has an invincible presence to it when you create in the magical power of invincibility.

You are creating this invincible shield around you right now. Allow the sense of invincibility to manifest with you now.

"I now allow myself to be an invincible being with 'All Truth.'"
"'All Truth' creates a sword of truth and I become invincible to others demands on my time and energy."
"The shield of invincibility is around me now."
"I am an invincible being."
"I am 'All Truth' now."

Right now you are reshaping and redefining your own identity to really believe in all you ever were. The essence of all you ever were brings with it a sense of truth for the mystery. The mystery re-creates and reforms itself continually, making you the power being you are. This energy brings with it truth, magic and power. Truth, magic and power create your determination to make "you" unbelievably strong in dealing with all patterns of fear around you, including others fears, directed toward you. You must now really focus on you, and get your own fears met directly by just knowing "All Truth" dissolves fear, and transmutes it to pure light of nothingness, where all dissolves and reforms again. Flow with this magical energy now. Flow with this essence. It is your gift to yourself.

"All Truth" enacts mystery. The mystery of "All Truth" is in bringing to your world your own discovery of yourself. This discovery of yourself is a truth-filled experience. Allowing the discovery of your truth to bring you all you need allows you now to really tap into a rich reservoir of power that receiving brings. Receiving brings gifts of empowerment. Empowered people receive. They are open to opportunities. They are abundant and they manifest all they need. Opportunity can only come when people allow themselves to receive. "All Truth" is a receiving process.

"I allow myself to receive through 'All Truth.'"

There is no wrong experience. "All Truth" is a receiving experience.

Allowing the absoluteness of "All Truth" to create a vortex in your energetic matrix and grid aligns you to the Earth and the stellar energies. This energy brings with it a sense of real and lasting power. There is a sense of absolute solidity and order in everything. Everything has solidity and order because everything is solid. You are allowing solidity and order to bring you all you ever were and will be. This is time to really announce to yourself that you have *friends* who help "you" create this *magical essence now*. You are allowing the solidity and order to create with you all that you need for your magical life of all you ever were. Bring this magic, this solidity to you now.

"All Truth" creates a sense of raw absolute power. Nothing else matters except the energy of who you are. Nothing else is important, and your own energy glints like steel or like a diamond, sharp and dense at the same time. You are allowing this sense of direction to shape you now. This direction brings with it power, for "All Truth" has the power to shape you and cut through illusion. Your relationship with it brings you into alignment with all you ever were and your relationship has encoded in it this power. Shape yourself now and cut through your illusion.

"All Truth" now creates a raw vortex of power to really strike at emotional and mind body pain. You are releasing all aspects of your former self in the new reality of "All Truth" now.

"All Truth" is a magical raw vortex of power, light and truth. Create with this magic now as you bring to your world the essence of all you ever were and will be. Right now this encodement brings peace.

Right now the Black Heart of "All Truth" brings to you the mystery of truth. Truth has encoded in it "All." The "All" of everything. Allowing the "All" of every living thing to create with you in the mystery for truth brings truth to you, in a way you can never imagine. You are resurrecting your own power and light to enact truth and mystery. This is a time to create a vortex of absoluteness for everything and everyone. You are resurrecting your own essence in this mystery now.

The resurrection of yourself in this mystery brings peace, light and power to you right now. Allowing peace, power and light to create with you is all you need to feel as the Black Heart of "All Truth" becomes encoded in your cellular memory. Allowing this process to create with you brings power, power, and power.

"All Truth" now expresses itself in really creating with the flow of just knowing; you have the weapons to fight any dark forces, which may attach themselves to you through your own fears. You are feeling and flowing in this energy now as you bring to your world a sense of real truth for the mystery.

The mystery has encoded in it all you ever were and will be, you are releasing all previously held patterns of fear around any aspect of yourself right now as you bring the simple truth and power to your being right now. Just feeling this energy brings you all you ever were. Allow the power of "All Truth" to create with you all you ever were.

"All Truth" allows the essence of The Feminine to be balanced with the Masculine. There is a need to really feel the fire and essence of The Feminine merge in oneness with The Masculine now. The merging takes place in the Black Heart—the point of singularity. The new creation begins here. Right now you are at a point where this mergence brings you to the point of absoluteness for everything. The point of absoluteness brings with it the energy essence and life force of every living thing to balance and redefine the energies of power. You are coalescing in this energy form now, as you refine and develop your own energetic relationship with all there is. This is time now for this mergence, this totality to really create with you, all you need to claim authority over the balance in your Feminine and Masculine centres.

The true balance of the Feminine and Masculine lies in the center of the Heart, the Black Heart, and the Earth's Heart.

"Hearts of "All" unite in this mergence now."

"All Truth" carries a sword of magic. There is magic in "All Truth" being enacted. Witnessing "All Truth" brings this magical sword to you to complete all you ever were in your ability to manifest your dreams. You are saying, "yes" to everything in your life, which brings you this power, life force and energy. You are allowing this power to create with you and you are one with this power now. Allow the source energy of all you ever were to manifest for you now. You are one with this essence now.

"All Truth" brings to your identity a sense of complete and permanent peace. Living with a peace-filled heart allows you to really allow yourself the gift of complete and total abundance for everything you choose to manifest. Energy is a manifestable thing. Summoning "All Truth" is a manifestable energy. Manifesting energy brings power, raw magical power to bring you all you need to feel, see, taste, smell and hear truth. Bring abundance to your heart now; true abundant hearts of "All Truth" unite now in celebration of the mystery.

Embodying The Divine Masculine of All Truth, Through The High Priest

"All Truth" embodies the power, essence and magical intention of who "you" are in "your" totality. This totality brings with it the source power of all you ever were and will be. The essence of this power has at its heart "you."

The essence, the seed of truth brings peace, space and order to every living aspect of your humanness, as you allow your power and light to create with you. Just feeling this now allows the essence of all you ever were to create with you in magic and wonder for who "you" are.

Your mighty intelligence is being encoded with "All Truth," as "All Truth" ignites the power and Feminine fire of your truth; allow this magic to create with you all you need for your magical life.

Right now the feeling of creating with "All Truth" brings a mighty rush of energy to you. This rush of energy has at its source, a sense of true power and respect for the mystery of all you ever were. You are vibrating to this rush, this power and this magic now.

Flow with it and surrender to the all of truth in every single aspect of your humanness now. You will feel a sense of mighty power in your cellular remembering. All the power of your own remembering is conferred upon you now, as you create in the mystery.

The mystery is your story, your truth and your beingness. The mystery allows you the space, peace and light to grow with you. This growth is conferred upon you as you open your heart to all there is. You are allowing this magical energy to bring you all you need to create a world of absoluteness in every living thing. "All Truth" brings to you a sense of absolute completeness in everything.

Right now the spirit of love brings the call of the "All Truth" beings to you. The sense of reflecting on what you really want for your life brings you to a point of knowing you are able to create a world of absoluteness in everything. You are flowing with the energy of completeness now, and there is a sense of openness to all life offers you. This sense of openness and trust creates a mergence and wonder for all you have to experience in your life right now. Just creating in this magical essence brings with it all the wonder of what you are capable of achieving in one incarnation.

You are vibrating to the sense of wonder, truth and joy; every moment is a miracle to trust the source of this remembering. Feeling the flow in this remembering brings you the essence of all you are, were and will be. You are a part of this mystery, this truth, when you part the veil and reveal your own truth to yourself.

"All Truth" brings to you now a feeling of absolute remembrance for the energy of love. The energy of love must be a tangible thing in your life and the energy of love must find itself creating with you all the time. The sense of pure love and adventure is part of the awakening to "All Truth." This truth is part of the magic of who "you" are. The magic of who "you" are just merges in oneness for all there is. Merging in oneness for all there is creates a vortex of raw power around you now.

You must feel this power and magic of your newly created "self" merge into the portal of "All Truth" now. The portal of "All Truth" creates in the mystery. Allow the mystery of "you" to create with "you" now.

You are witnessing the joy and power of "All Truth" now, as you take yourself into the absoluteness of all you ever were. You are absoluting. Everything you experience is an absolute experience. The experience of absoluteness brings with it a sense of pure magic. Pure magic is in absoluteness. The absoluteness of life is absoluting. The sense of all, all of everything is in this source, this magical energy. Feel the magic of this source energy now.

"All Truth" brings to you now a profound sense of knowing there is no turning back in your life. No turning back brings you to a point of just flowing with the energy of all there is. Flowing with this energy allows you now to really create a world of knowing you are able to bring to your world the sense of real joy for the mystery of your creations.

This is your birth right and your belief in your own capacity to really create a world of pure love and light for the mystery of yourself. Never see yourself in the struggle to understand life. You are just in the mystery all the time you are part of it now. To seek "All Truth" brings you into complete resonance with all there is.

"All Truth" is being embodied in you now, as you create a world of pure light and truth for the mystery. The mystery of allowing the "All Truth" guides to be embodied creates in your heart's intelligence another weapon to fight your own dark shadow.

You are allowing this sense of pure truth for all you are bring you to the point of pure love and truth for the mysteries. The essence of pure love and truth creates in you now a bonfire of cosmic energy, as the darkness from within you is released quickly and completely. You are allowing the embodiment of us to forward you at a very important part of your soul's evolvement.

You are now feeling the essence of "All Truth" become an embodiment of your own belief in the totality of your humanness. The totality of your humanness has encoded in it the most incredible light, power and energy. You are witnessing this restructuring now, as the simple truth of all there ever was right now.

You are restructuring every single emotion you have ever had about anybody. This can be easily felt and seen by them. This energy brings with it the belief in your own power to create a world of love and truth for all you ever were.

Just allow this energy now to reshape every single experience and event you are being shown now. This vibration matches nothing like anything else you have ever experienced.

You are forwarding this vibration exponentially when you create with this magical energy. Truly the rare alchemical magical energy gets so powerful and you are just vibrating and allowing it to create a world of truth and light for all you are capable of right now.

Just trusting this sacred sequence of events to unfold around you, as they are holy acts, and you need to see them as this. You are allowing yourself now the essence of all you were to bring you this peace and light. Trust in the power it brings you and your world.

"All Truth" brings a rare sense of order in everything. "All Truth" brings a rare alchemical experience to you when you allow the preciousness of who you are to create with you. This is a time now to really create with this preciousness now. Allowing the source of "All" reveals "All." The "All" is the call. The "All" is the call to the great ones to guide your every moment, and see every moment as a rare and loving moment to embrace power, energy and light. Feel this now and embrace this now.

The vibration of alchemy creates with "All Truth." The vibration of the true alchemical process brings with it a sense of pure power for the mystery. You are flowing with this energy now, and you are bathed in it.

The sense of "who" you are brings you now into a co-creation with all there is, as a truth of "who you are" creates with you now. This energy is oneness. Oneness, peace and order. Allowing the spirit of all there is creates with you now, as you are now, you are vibrating to the essence, energy and oneness of every living thing.

Right now the essence of "All Truth," the kernel of it creates with you in its splendour and glory. The essence and energy of "All Truth" keeps you in a space of suspension to allow you to make the leap, to bring you your power and light. Power and light create magic and your magical life just keeps getting more powerful when you acknowledge to yourself you are able to really feel this freedom and power.

The essence of freedom and power is in knowing you are able to hold all and keep all for your abundance. "All Truth" is an abundance energy, because "All Truth" magnetizes the right people, circumstances and frequencies to you. This vibration holds you now. This vibration holds you in your heart. You are vibrating to "All Truth" as an abundant energy now, just an abundant energy now.

You are now allowing "All Truth" to bring to you magic and fire. There is magic and fire in "All Truth." You are receiving the essence of magic and fire with "All Truth." Right now the essence energy and life force brings with it a sense of pure absoluteness in everything you have created. Creating in the magic and fire of "All Truth" brings a true sense of peace and love. Flowing in this energy now allows this peace and light to bring you all you need to love. This is time to really allow love to flow through "All Truth."

Right now feeling the need to really embody "All Truth" is allowing you a sense of peace, space and order in everything. Peace, space and order create oneness; oneness is the state of acceptance of all there ever was, and will be. Accepting this reality, this totality, creates in you mergence and light. Mergence and light bring this power, this magic to you. Allow the mergence to create with you now in oneness for all life.

"All Truth" brings solidarity. Your solidarity with yourself grows when "All Truth" becomes encoded in your central core matrix. Your total belief in all you are capable of allows you to partake in the miracle of who "you" are and drive this miracle to all your dreams.

Keep dreams grounded. Earth dreams. They are only clouds in the sky unless they are earthed. Keep earthing dreams. All dreams need to be earthed. Get practical. Get real. Earth the truth. It cannot manifest unless it is earthed. Allow yourself now to fully earth your own dreams by knowing "All Truth" supports and protects you. Feel this now.

Your energy must encompass "All Truth" as a way of being human. You have seen with your energy that you are now forwarding your own essence and truth and living in this truth and energy. The shift has had a profound effect on your reality. You are now ready to receive and you are allowing this receiving to bring you power, power and more power. It's all about personal power, which can only come from the light of your new beginning. You are allowing now all you ever were to really create with you now. You are strong and very powerful indeed.

Feeling the power and strength of "All Truth" brings to your heart the essence of all it is to be human. Humanness brings with it a sense of complete surrender to all there is. Surrendering to all there is; is a magical energy. You are now flowing with it and you must feel the essence, energy and life force of it create with you now, as you begin to allow the joy and peace of your new life to bring you all you need to love.

The essence of "All Truth" is in the magic of allowing "you." Your own magical heart creates with you continuously. The "All Truth" vibration opens up the doorway to this reality now.

"Heart I Love You."

Feeling now the essence, energy and power of all you are capable of brings you to the space of absoluteness in everything.

Why shouldn't absoluteness be absolute?

Why shouldn't you, the human, experience the absoluteness of everything in your world?

This is a time to really explore this sense of real and permanent happiness. This real and permanent peace and light.

Allow, allow, allow.

"All Truth" now speaks of awareness of possibilities that exist for all humans at this time. The possibilities are endless for creation, and the possibilities bring with them a sense of absoluteness in every living thing.

You are absoluting, and in absoluting you are drawing powerful new energy to you right now. Absoluting is a term to define you; your own belief that it is all absolutely perfect in your world. All is absolutely perfect and bountiful, absolutely perfect.

You are absoluting when you give no energy to any past aspect of yourself, which interferes with your own core belief in creating your own absolutely perfect world.

This absolutely perfect world would bring with it a sense of truth for the mystery; the absolute truth for the mystery. Feeling this and bringing it into resonance with your truth is the sum total of all you ever were, the absolute sum total of every living thing.

Begin the journey to absoluting now.

"All Truth" speaks of allowing your own sense of absoluteness to be your guide. Your guide is this perfect place of synchronicity where past, present and future merge into oneness for all there is. This past, present and future merge in the still point, the unified field, the Black Heart. Allowing this radiance to create with you now brings you into a relationship with your power.

Your power is your relationship with "All"; every living has "All" encoded in it. You are absoluting into this reality and creating in this reality now. Creating in the absoluting of all you ever were is just so powerful right now. You are absoluting right now.

Creating in the fire of this new heart; let her burn brightly. Let her see you and all you ever were and will be. This is your role now.

You are now bringing to your world the sense of raw passion and truth for all there is. Raw passion and truth bring light and your world now must bring to you, your own belief in all you ever were.

Allowing this energy to manifest with you brings you to the source of every living thing. Every living thing has its source in the creative aspect of "All Truth." "All Truth" creates this sense of awareness and allowance of "All." "All" is everything. You are the "All" of it "All."

The "All Truth" guides now bring the essence of release. The essence of *release* is to finally *surrender* to a part of yourself that creates in the magical energy of all there ever was.

This energy brings with it a knowing that you are now able to create in the world of all your ever were. This world allows now for peace and light to enfold you and enclose you. There is a sense now of this magic and light bringing you all you need for your love-filled life. This life creates continually. Continuous love and energy pour in when the flow establishes itself. There is a mergence in this flow. There is also a sense of knowing "All Truth" supports the mergence of every living thing. Feel the flow, creating with it, brings raw alchemical power to everything in your life. You are love now.

"All Truth" is the sum total of allowing you, your own immortal self, bring you to the point of absoluteness for every living thing. The point of absoluteness for every living thing brings with it magic and light. Magic and light for your immortal life. The essence of this magical forgiveness brings with it peace and light. Peace and light allow the spirit of all you ever were to create with you in wonder for all there is.

This sense of wonder brings with it power, power, power. Your life is a testament to this living power, when you tap into this rich vein of abundance. Feeling abundance all around you and embracing the world of abundance awes you right now. Raw magical power. Raw magical power to create the life of perfect peace and magic for all there is. *"Heart I love you, Heart I love you."*

Allow the spirit of your own power to manifest. "All Truth" manifests through sound. "All Truth" is created through sound. The energy of sound is part of what you are bringing to your life right now. As you embrace and birth your new world right now you are forming this magical energy. This energy has at its heart your own belief in all you are capable of right now. Allow the spirit of who "you" are to create with you in wonder for all you are and ever will be. The essence, energy and life force is unbelievable. You are opening up to this energy right now. Receive the abundance it brings.

"All Truth" creates in the vortex of absoluteness where all of life brings to you the gift of your humanness. This is a time for this magical creation to merge with you in totality for all there is. Allowing this totality to merge with you brings you peace, space and order now.

The essence of this order has at its heart, the very core, the absoluteness of every living thing. The absoluteness of every living thing is the sum total of truth for the mystery. Truth for the mystery creates peace, power and light for all there is. Peace, power and light for all there is, is in the allowance and light for the sacred creation of yourself. The sacred creation of yourself is in mergence and oneness with the alchemical process of sound, with the consciousness of this sound merging into oneness with all life. Allow this to be creating with you right now.

"All Truth" brings to you now the essence, energy and life force of all you ever were as you merge into the knowing that you are allowing this mighty magic to bring you all you need to love. You are feeling the fire and power of this energy to create with you all the time. The essence, energy and life force brings with it all you ever were and will be. This essence has at its heart truth for the mystery. The mystery of allowing "you" the power and light of all you ever were. Feeling this now shapes your reality and you know your reality has only one consideration, this energy, this light and this power.

"All Truth" brings this and more.

"All Truth" brings ancient sacred laws to you and these laws are invisible forces that bring you power in your whole totality. Feeling this now brings you closer to the essence and heart of yourself.

"Heart I love you."

Your energy with "All Truth" brings you now to a point of no return in your cellular remembering. This energy brings to you now the energy of all there ever was, as you create in the vortex of "All Love and All Truth."

This is a time for remembering this truth and light. Understanding and feeling this brings you now to the heart of all you ever were. Just feel now the heart of all you ever were. This vibration has encoded in it your own soul's matrix and within it, it is complete.

There is a sense of completeness now with this energy. You are vibrating to this energy right now in your soul's creation. Your soul's matrix is encoded in "All Truth." Experience the expression of it now.

"Heart I love you."
"Hearts truth I receive your sacred laws."
"My soul's matrix is encoded in "All Truth." Experience the expression of this now."

"All Truth" now allows power to be earthed, for "All Truth" is a powerful manifester. Your relationship with "All Truth" keeps growing when you create all you need with it. By intoning: *"In the name of All Truth"* you clear the pathway to your power and light to bring you all you need for your "truth-filled" life. This truth-filled way of being human creates protection for you to journey into a space within yourself that knows it anyway and keeps you safe no matter what happens. You are allowing "you" now to really merge into oneness with all there is and this mergence brings with it a sense of light and ownership of your creations.

"All Truth" is a vortex; a vortex of energy, actually, "All Truth" brings energy. Energy is a renewable resource. It is infinite. Energy is an infinite renewable resource, and it is at your fingertips. It creates a special relationship with the heart of truth. All energy sources create through the power and light of the renewable resource of "All Truth" in their purest alchemical force. This force creates with it; all there is and will be. Allowing this renewable energy source to create with you all you need to bring to your life, magic and peace. Allow this magic and peace to bring you now all you need to love.

Feeling the heart of "All Truth" is an alchemical force. Feeling this heart, this essence allows the forces of all you ever were just create in you the absolute divine essence of all you ever were, for who are you if you cannot really give this gift back to yourself? This sense of real allowance for this process, this alchemical process, this vitalizing force brings with it all the magnificence and light of your truth.

This vibration is in this allowance, this allowance of the allowance.

When does allowance become allowed in your life?
When does the essence of your allowance bring with it the
essence, energy and vitalizing force of all there is?

Feeling this force, this light, this energy just brings you this extraordinary power and ability to say:

"Yes, this really is mine. This really is allowed by me."
"Heart I love you, Truth."

"All Truth" allows now the true aspect of all there ever was to create with you in wonder for all there is in the universe and beyond. Look beyond the ordinary, the mundane and the mortal to the immortal truth and light of all there ever was.

This is your time to celebrate the consciousness of this new form of yours. True energy and light right now, you must celebrate and cherish your power and mystery, for "All Truth" gives you this and more. Allowing this special magic and light to envelope you creates the magic and essence of all you were.

"All Truth" creates in you now the simple pure trust that all you ever will be creates with you in the mystery. The essence of the mystery is just that, the mystery. You are alive to the enormous potential of the mystery now, as you envelope yourself in pure light and joy for all there is. Creating in this energy brings you all you ever were, and will be.

The essence, energy and life force re-creates itself with you as you awaken to the potential of all you ever were and will be. This allowance has encoded in it, power and light. Power and light brings truth, space and order.

Feeling the energy of "All Truth" brings to the now the simple joy of all there is. This simple joy has at its heart, the essence of all you ever were and will be. "All Truth" is a statement of deservability about what you are capable of in your life right now. The statement of truth has at its core your own sacred essence and truth for all there is.

This is allowing you the peace and light of all you ever were to envelope you now, and you need to feel the essence of you truth and light with "All Truth." The statement of truth lives in cellular remembering. Cellular remembering brings truth to the surface, and truth is the great teacher. Allow your teacher—Truth—"All Truth," to guide you now. You are love.

"All Truth" now whispers to you the sense of completion. The energy of completion is upon you right now, as a cycle of infinity has been encoded on your cellular memory. This is a time to celebrate and feel the essence, energy and life force of completion in every stage of your journey. Just feeling this now allows you peace, space and order in your life.

The energy of peace, space and order is encoded on you when you complete a project, a life and a world. Everything has in your life now this totality, this peace, this space and this order.

Allow yourself now to know this transmission is complete, for you have completed your journey with the study and experience of "All Truth."

Allow this companion, "All Truth" to guide you.

"All Truth" is a shining sword that illuminates all.

"All Truth" restores, shares and brings hope and peace to all you ever were and will be. Rest now in the knowledge that you have been initiated and you are free to embrace the world of "All Truth" and live the principles of "All Truth."

Thank you
The "All Truth" Guides

Part II:
The High Priest

Introduction to The High Priest

Who is The High Priest?

The High Priest is an inspirational archetype/role model for men and women in today's society who respect everything a balanced person needs to live a detached, powerful and love-filled life. The word High Priest in our contemporary world means a person who seeks the height of wisdom and knowledge. A Priest is a seeker of truth. A Priest seeks truth and applies it to the everyday world. (Not to be confused with the religious clergy of priests who may or may not embrace this truth.)

Bringing in the power of the creative masculine through The High Priest destroys the patriarchal system. It's like lifting off layer upon layer of cruelty and hatred to all people who try and allow their new soul to explore their totality, in human form.

The High Priest allows you to explore your creative masculine, examining the external reality through patriarchy. You are challenging your need to use this model, which through control will eventually destroy itself.

About Part II of this Book:

Carmel Glenane explores core issues in men and women's lives from relationships, power, love, self-responsibility for their creative masculine.

The High Priest challenges in a practical yet revolutionary way your core identity through the creative masculine. Primarily addressed to men, the work becomes gender inclusive throughout the chapters. These teachings were given life after my teaching tour to Egypt in late 2006, where I was instructed to birth my own inner creative masculine.

All channeled material is purely subjective until it is tested against "reality" (i.e. others outside yourself). With clients and students in my practice I tested this material bringing through the energy of my own High Priest in healings. I began creating this energy of The High Priest in initiations and case studies of men and women who have been initiated. Both men and women requested initiations to balance and to strengthen their own masculine identity in a culture, which does not respect the true masculine principle.

It has taken seven years to complete this book. It challenged every belief my culture and world presented me with in my creative masculine identity.

As you read this section of the book, you may begin to notice that The High Priest can challenge some "core" issues around relationship patterning. I suggest seeking professional help if you feel you need further work on some of these issues. It is strongly recommended that you seek support for your journey as you are being initiated into a new way of being human.

This book is an initiatory process. The creative masculine vibration opens your heart, bringing balance and truth, awakening your intelligent heart.

The High Priest

These transmissions first began after my fifth teaching tour to Egypt in late 2006 and embrace the teachings from Ancient Mystery School traditions including Atlantean and Egyptian, through the Philosophy of the Divine Feminine and The Atlantis Rising Mystery School Guides.

The High Priest speaks of power: The High Priest is allowing his power to be part of your consciousness now. With my power you can go beyond yourself. You can challenge your definition of what your masculine "self" is. Your masculine self is a representation of your creative masculine, which is enacted, in human form. With me you have power. You have power to give to another to protect another and to create with another.

The High Priest embodies the sacred principles of duality. He has many roles assigned to him. These roles are served in his pursuit of Divine Truth. The High Priest must be in pursuit of this ideal for his whole life. He must guard against his own fears of being de-powered. He must stand alone knowing "he" is able to withstand emotional slavery others place on him. He will not be in the presence of emotional attachments, which see him in any way a victim of another's expectation of him. His role is a sacred one; he carries truth, he carries truth through power. Through controlling his emotions and his rigid mind, he brings to a woman his protection, power and love. He loves deeply and powerfully. He is the sword of truth. He is with you now.

CHAPTER 1

The High Priest Speaks

Carmel: Who are you and how can you help people create what they need in our world today?

The High Priest: The High Priest creates through truth. The High Priest is an archetype of masculine energy which has its beginning in the ancient mystery schools which were temples to provide order, stability and spiritual discipline to a community, city and country. In creating with a High Priest, you will begin to tap into and explore these ancient, long-forgotten secrets and wisdom.

In doing this you will begin to find that you are creating a world for yourself as a person, which will see you being able to enact the true masculine function, and to find yourself in your own power. Your inner masculine will become realized and you will begin to see your world in a balanced way, free from the enslavement your society places on you to act and behave in a certain way.

Your society has placed a barrier on you to create in your masculine power, because of its demands on you to function in purely an economic framework, and not a spiritual or balanced way to enact your inner masculine, and create the person you know yourself to be.

Carmel: I have been teaching and healing men through my practice for many years and have observed that many men seem very reluctant to embrace the emotional world that women do. What can The High Priest do to help?

The High Priest: The High Priest will show men that they are allowed to experience emotions in a way that is respectful of their truth: A man must be able to do this if he is to create in his own psyche this inner equilibrium. Men are generally terrified of not having emotional authority in relationships. The world of female emotions creates in him a distaste of the mess the emotional world has to offer: It is beyond his control; he cannot control the emotional landscape of women, other men and children who lose control. Men must be able to recognize that within themselves they too have the same emotions. To say men don't have emotions is just castrating. Men must recognize…

"Yes I have emotions, too. I must nurture myself in recognizing these emotions, and not feel fearful of them."

Carmel: I don't feel many men really know or even understand the word "self nurture." Could you please explain the word/term "self nurture" and how it applies to men?

The High Priest: The High Priest is a man who understands what it is to be a man and respects that source of his manhood. What it is to be a man in one society differs from another society (i.e. tribal, urban or rural life). Basically a man needs to recognize that he has a specific function in the choosing of his sex, and that is to see himself first as being able to control his own desire to have control in all of life. Men are conditioned to have control in all of life. They are fearful of losing their manhood if they don't have control (i.e. generally boys are conditioned not to cry as children).

You need to see this pattern emerging in your society more and more. There isn't an inner balance in the way men move in and out of their world. Their world is the mind and control. Women deal with emotions. "Men" deal with the "big things" — control and order.

Control for its own sake is dangerous. To control is to be extremely fearful of allowing synchronicities to happen, psychic ability to develop, and the ability to just stay still and contemplate all around you. Control is the weapon, and men use it ruthlessly in your society, and in doing so, are not in the true spirit of surrendering to their higher truth.

Carmel: *Both men and women seem then to be in the same pattern. They both want control.*

The High Priest: Yes, de-powered people always want control. However men must be ruthless on themselves in saying

"Why do I want to control all the time? What do I really want out of this need to control all the time?"

It is the definition of control that needs to be considered here. Men need to be able to say much more,

"I don't need to 'control' this relationship," for it is in relationships that men find it so difficult to lose control.

Carmel: *What exactly will a person gain by being initiated to the vibration of The High Priest?*

The High Priest: He will gain surrender and not feel he has to be a certain type of man your society portrays him as being. He will gain strength and power by being connected to this source of balanced masculine power. He will gain mastery over his emotions, which see him as having to have all the answers, having to behave a certain way, to "act as a man" and more importantly respect the source of all life, which is The Feminine Principle.

Carmel: Explain The Feminine Principle and how it applies to men now in our society?

The High Priest: You need to see The Feminine Principle as being one of love for the whole of life; the whole of life is the feminine structure. The feminine structures the world. The world, our mother earth is feminine. The earth is a mother, she is cyclical, she can be destructive, to make way for the new. Your men are desecrating the feminine structure, the earth, by their need to control all the time. There must be a respect for The Feminine Principle in life, and that is a respect for all life. To create a new belief in what being a man is, will require rigorous effort for a man who wants to work under a banner of truth. It's just that simple. For a man to create in his truth, he must have balance in all of his life. The Western world really does not support or allow a man this structure or freedom. "For men," it is in recognizing this. Men must recognize that they must create a truthful life if they want to embody the principles of becoming a High Priest in your society.

Carmel: Create in truth: What exactly does this mean?

The High Priest: To create in truth means trusting in the processes of being human and allowing the human self time to begin to know what you must do to be a man. You know men are just too afraid to examine some fundamental beliefs about themselves, their role in their society and their relationships.

Carmel: What exactly are these fundamental beliefs?

The High Priest: Structuring and ordering: Men need more support in structuring and ordering; the energy of structure is very important. A man must be able to structure and order himself. A man is an order creator. He creates order. He has a firm definition of what he must do to create order and structure in his life. He needs to observe this much more in himself and this world.

Carmel: How practically can a man apply this structuring and ordering without controlling?

The High Priest: Yes, structuring and ordering is a knowing that a man has a belief about himself, and what he must do with his life. He has created a space in this inner landscape, which isn't controlling another in anyway. For this is against his definition of himself.

Carmel: I'm now trying to make sure that men who are reading this transmission really know what this means as a definition of being a High Priest, perhaps you could help me here?

The High Priest: Yes, you are not allowing the forces of the higher self or soul to co-create here. There is within every man a knowing of really what it is to be a man and within that there is a respect for who he is. Each and every man knows this. It's part of his genetic, race and cultural definition of himself.

Carmel: How can a man create with The High Priest?

The High Priest: A man's creative function (like a woman's) is his essence. Without a personal creative function, a man cannot define who he is. A man is known to himself as a creator: I create. This is who I am. The High Priest activates the creative process in a man. A man becomes an expressive creative being with The High Priest. He actually creates and in doing so shapes his destiny. The High Priest makes him a creative man. It allows or ignites the spark of creation to be lit.

Carmel: What would The High Priest like to communicate with the readers?

The High Priest: Control. You must really try and understand your definition of control and what you are trying to do with your lives. You are curious about the ancient priesthood, sure, now you must start sifting through all the layers of the definitions, which have controlled the name High Priest. Your communities have priests, you must not confuse the Ancient Teachings and The Bearers of Light with the enslavement the word "priesthood" has in your world.

You must be very clear about this, and you must not try and assume the Ancient Priesthood is in anyway part of the corrupt world this ancient lineage has been subjected to.

Jesus Christ and the masters of all spiritual traditions have had to suffer for bringing their truth to this Earth, only to have their sacred priesthood deconsecrated by demons that use this name to gain power over weak souls who want light and hope.

The Priesthood is the ancient lineage of light for human kind. By attuning now to the pure essence of the priesthood and what it means, you will be attacked by energies of priest frequencies, which have de-powered the sacred flame of truth. Stand up, under the light of the Ancient Priesthood and do not confuse it with anything baser.

The Ancient Priesthood is exactly that, Ancient. The ancientness of the Priesthood makes it sacred. Its sacred energy is its truth. The lineage you are responding to is an ancient one; the ancient world is what the definition of the priesthood really means. The ancient world energies offer the modern world travelers of spirituality security and reliability. Our secrets have stood the test of time.

Our secrets are the Bearers of Truth. All truth lies in the Ancient Mysteries of creation. So, why do you ask, were the ancients so corrupted by their priesthood? The ancient priesthood was corrupt, yes. It was corrupt. In this corruption/chaos, order is created and restored.

A corrupt Priesthood creates a corrupt world, city and country. Look at your own corrupt Priesthood. Look at those who espouse truth through their words. Do their actions match words? Through the understanding of the mysteries of the ancient world, you will create a connection with the feminine energies, which reflect the whole priest.

The "whole" priest is not corrupt, because he has addressed the feminine principle, which is the essence of all life.

Creating power is the essential task of the High Priest. Creating power and maintaining equilibrium of truth must be maintained at all times. For men wishing to create with this energy frequency they must have at their core identity, a desire for truth and stability in their own world.

They have looked at the world around them and know its corruption. The world of men is one of corruption. The High Priest seeks to address this within himself. He knows the value of balanced detachment. He knows no fear of this truth. This truth is his best weapon against corruption. His truth is his salvation, because it is only by truth that his world, the world he has created will evolve.

A man must allow himself the sensation of power in his capacity to feel what he needs to bring to his world pure truth. It is just that simple.

A powerful man is a truth-seeker and he will not compromise. To create power for a man is to create a profound love of the sacred mysteries.

The ancient sacred mysteries are his sword of truth. His sword of truth is the mystery of creation and the essence of his manhood must be the pursuit of this truth. Sharpen your weapons. Shape your truth, men. *What will it be?* Truth wins over corruption.

To create in the frequency of love will enable a man to really follow this dream of pursuing truth. You must, as a man, create with the energy of absolute truth in everything. This time is your time to create with the mystery of love, for love brings to your soul, truth.

To begin at the beginning now, is to recognize that without the energy of love, you cannot create truth.

Carmel: What is love to a man seeking truth to become a High Priest?

The High Priest: Love for this man is to be in presence of his own sacred Divine Feminine self, so in this space of trust for his own Feminine Nature, is the nature of self-nurturing.

Carmel: Let's look at the nature of self nurturing for a man wanting the challenge of creating with The High Priest.

The High Priest: The nature of self-nurturing brings to a man a profound shift in the way he sees himself. He now requires that "he" see himself in this truth. This truth is to recognize that he must discard the energy of self-indulgence in what your culture/society expects from a man.

Carmel: Please explain his "Self Indulgence" further.

The High Priest: Men tend to indulge their belief that they are the controllers in society. They indulge this too much and often don't take into consideration the value of honoring the forces of the Feminine to create with. If they could honor the forces of the Feminine, they would not expect their world to be solely their own creation.

Carmel: So it's "I create, so therefore I am?"

The High Priest: Absolutely and it has been for as long as men have ignored their own capacity to really value themselves and who they truly are as opposed to how your society perceives a man as being, and through this society, how he perceives himself as being. The High Priest brings to his world his own inner order, the discipline to trust the truth of his heart. His heart is his truth center, and a barometer for his true masculine identity. The true masculine identity cannot be crafted without a solid understanding of his heart's nature. The nature of the heart must be above all else. All men should meditate on the nature of what the heart wants. For it is then that a man will find his connection with his truth. His heart is this beginning and this relationship with his heart must come before everything else. Nothing must come before what his heart tells him to do.

You may find yourself being initiated at this point.

Carmel: In my personal journey, while writing the Divine Masculine, I was initiated when a small cockroach became trapped in my ear. I awoke to the piercing buzzing sound of a cockroach trapped in my left ear canal, (the feminine side). The symology of a cockroach symbolizes to me the energy of the Ancient Egyptian scarab, a beetle of immortality, which was blocking my ability to "listen" to my feminine self. Following an emergency 3 a.m. visit to the local hospital to unsuccessfully remove the insect, I was forced to return home to rest and integrate. During this time I fully surrendered to the fact that I may lose my hearing. In fact, I did not lose my hearing and for three days I used ear candles to release the dying insect. The initiation I feel was showing me that I needed to open up to the inner ear of the "masculine" through my right ear. Finally, I realized that the Priests were trying to communicate this to me.

Carmel: What would you like to communicate with me now?

The High Priest: For The High Priest there is a need to really bring truth to every situation. He must always be truthful to himself. There is a real need for a man to honor his truth. This truth must be above all else. There is something vital missing in a man who cannot honor this part of his nurturing. For a High Priest there must be the need to accept his truth as an everyday aspect of his reality.

Carmel: In what way, practically, can a man do this?

The High Priest: At a practical level a man must do this by observing his thoughts and how these thoughts apply to himself and his everyday world. He must remember that all thoughts are transmitters and that thoughts transmit electrical energy or charges. The energetic vibration also needs to be considered when a man is working with his truth.

Carmel: Is his energetic charge, vibration something one must be aware of as well?

The High Priest: Yes, because the vibration holds truth for a man as well. The vibration holds and carries truth.

The High Priest must carry truth to create new meaning for his life and for humanity to do this there is a need to allow the frequency of truth to be around him through the energy of love. Love is the energy that carries truth and love is the energy, which creates truth.

Love is the most important ingredient for the truth to be realized. To create in love The High Priest must carry the vibration of love, for all love is the barometer, which will determine how the Priest will evolve.

It is very important now to just create this loving vibration by monitoring all reactions, which interfere with the energy of love. All energies, which interfere with this loving vibration, will disrupt The High Priest's journey to his "self" for the "self" of any man cannot be made truthful without love. Love will bring the reward of trust in The High Priest's truth.

To begin to find the love is to be in the presence of your own heart and to see it as an organism, which needs care.

Say to yourself: *"I love my heart."* Then breathe the truth of your heart into yourself at any time. This is important now to create through this vibration of love. To create through the vibration of love is to really feel peaceful and love filled toward yourself, every part of yourself at all times.

The High Priest's role is one of creative loving. Creative loving for The High Priest is one of letting go of his definition of what love is. For love, create with the present act of creation.

The High Priest is a figure of power and strength when he combines this act of loving for himself. There is an acknowledgement of the masculine process and what is involved in this process to begin to create.

It is very important to really find what your definition of the masculine is and create with this. You must really allow your true creative worth to be realized in the masculine process. All creative processes involve the masculine. The creative is active and masculine.

The masculine is a creative act. Really create with the masculine in the creative act. The masculine enacts, it creates, it makes whole. The masculine really is the fire of ascension. The fire of ascension is the creative act of the masculine.

All men need a strong and grounding relationship with what it is to create the masculine, for when they do they have a blueprint for what they must create in their life and world. Man must recognize why they have incarnated as men. This is to enact and create with the masculine.

How does a man do this? He does this by observing and noting all emotions that are negative around the masculine creative principle. Naturally, it is not easy in a culture, which abuses the masculine as much as the feminine to even know why this energy is taking place. Men don't realize that the culture they are part of, the patriarchal model, abuses the very thing a man needs to create his masculine. Men must observe very carefully in our culture just where they are allowing their creative masculine spirit, their fire to be absorbed into a vast vacuum of energy, which is not empowering them in their creative masculine.

It's just so simple. Men must breathe in their creative masculine every day and use breath of fire, to fire up their bellies. Fire energy keeps a man creating in the masculine and in truth for his masculine. Deep belly breathing, firing up the belly is essential for man to enact his creative masculine spirit. He must become the fire god. This exercise will help.

Exercise: Breathe deeply into your belly inhaling through your nostrils and feeling the belly rise and fall. Establish this deep breathing technique now. Feel the belly rise and fall like a balloon being inflated and then let down.

The deep belly breathing technique is ideally performed outside in the morning sunlight. The sun is life giving, creative and fires up the masculine powers. In deep belly breathing, you are breathing in the creative powers of the sun, inhaling this life giving energy into the belly then visualizing the belly as a golden fireball, as you push the fears and toxicity out.

Visualize the sun coming into the nostrils inhaling deeply, powerfully and rhythmically. The energy is opening up the belly now and the belly is now releasing stored toxicity and past patterns. This is now being returned to the sun as a gift or exchange to be transmuted into life giving prana. This cycle can be repeated eight times. Full benefit would be derived for 10 minutes, observing the breath and especially the emotion that surface. Intoning a mantra further re-codes the DNA to accept new frequencies for the masculine principle to be enacted.

Affirmations:
"I now accept my full masculine power."
"I now create with my full masculine power."
"I am now a creative masculine being."

The vibration of belly breathing will be felt in the spinal column and will be needed to strengthen the spine and bring in more life force to the spinal fluid. Strengthening the spine will also activate and strengthen the spinal vertebrae. A powerfully aligned spinal column creates vigor and life force for the masculine. To strengthen and align the spinal column, you will need to make a commitment to activating your masculine fire spirit through a series of visualization exercises to strengthen your commitment to your masculine power and creativity.

Chapter 2

Connecting with The High Priest

These exercises will begin to prepare you for being in the energy of your masculine power.

Spine Strengthening Visualization Exercise

Exercise: *You are deeply buried under the Earth. This earth is warm, nourishing, it is the void. It is alive, but empty, peaceful quiet and loving. You are deep in the belly of Mother Earth. Feel this now. Feel the warmth, the gentle rocking, swaying, of being in the mother's womb.*

You are suddenly awakening, stirring. Life is beginning. You feel your energy gathering momentum. This is allowing you to begin your ascent into the world. You feel yourself slowly emerging, your warm silky cocoon is being stretched and you now find yourself on the surface of the Earth, gazing at the eastern sunrise, pulsing its glory at you. You now feel yourself responding to this new form, your new self. You feel a stirring in your spine at the base of the spine (the coccyx). You perceive an energy attached to your spine. It is a force you may like to visualize, it is a scarab beetle. This scarab beetle has its source in the mother's belly like you and it has been sent to you to strengthen your masculine.

Begin your breathing sequence; breathe in. Feel the scarab moving, at the base of your spine. Its thread connects it to the Earth for its energy. Now it is travelling through your spinal column; it is in the marrow. Its strong wings and body are opening energy and shifting stagnancy in your newly emerging self.

Feel this now. Go to your spine: Imagine each vertebrae being opened up and aligned. Vertebra by vertebra. Each vertebra is responding to the call of life. Your scarab is working hard to create light and strength in your spinal column. Imagine your scarab turning red now bringing life force to this energy belt in your newly emerging self. Life force is being created; the scarab is squeezing out fluid to your spinal column.

You feel your spine activating, releasing energy blocked deep within the system. There is a boost to your energy fluid; feel your senses being strengthened.

You are beginning to feel raw power course up your spine. Breathe deeply, powerfully and rhythmically. Now allowing the energy to stabilize. You need now to visualize the energy belt turning bright orange. Really turn on the orange filter in your imagination. The scarab is now squeezing out bright orange liquid. Cleansing and invigorating energy is now travelling up your spine. You will find your immune system strengthened bringing a celebration of your sensuous self and an appreciation of your physical body. This energy is bringing drive and action to your spinal column; it is activating deeply held memory patterns. It is shifting out and dislodging stagnancy and limiting structures, like shit, being dissolved. Your spine becomes alive. Feel it glowing like a crimson sunset and traveling up the spine to capture the morning rays of the rising sun. Your whole spine is beginning to radiate with this energy of pure power. Visualize inner cleansing now.

Now your scarab has found its home, deep in your heart center. Breathe deeply, powerfully and rhythmically, feeling the scarab rest at your heart. Your scarab is now turning clockwise around your heart, beginning at the point of your heart, which would correspond to 6 o'clock. Your scarab is releasing rich emerald green energy going round in a circle until it reaches 6 o'clock again. Watch your scarab enact the mystery of creation as its progress is noted by you. Your scarab will stop when it feels you are ready for it to stop. You may see it cease its motion after three circles, or five or seven or even nine circles. The vibration of emerald will strengthen the muscles of your heart. Your heart will become stronger physically. You will begin to feel that you are physically rejuvenated. You will begin to feel expansion in your awareness, now; you will want to begin to experience new direction in your life.

By allowing your physical rejuvenation to open up your heart you will now feel as though your arms are expanding outward. Visualize your scarab's wings opening up from the heart center, gathering momentum and taking off. For this is what you are doing right now, taking off! Your heart is opening, you are expanding, and your heart is opening like the wings of a scarab beetle, each segment of wing, propelling you upward and outward. Your head is buzzing and your body is now feeling electric, powered up and ready for what you have to achieve in your life. Hold this energy for as long as you wish, maybe five minutes or even longer.

Now you may allow yourself to return to everyday awareness of yourself. Your flame has been glowing red hot in your heart. Now, return the heat to your base chakra and release anything you need to into the deep center of the Earth. This exercise can be done daily or whenever you feel you need energy.

To survive in the world you have created for yourself requires that you use all the aggression and anger your society has given you. You like this as it often feeds that part of yourself that is weak and vulnerable. In actual fact it is destroying the very thing you need to assume your power as a High Priest.

Your reality is being fed to you all the time and you are responding to that external reality, that false reality. Why don't you admit now that you have been fed a false reality and you do not like the world you have been shown? You are allowed to admit that you are not happy with your false world. You can admit this to yourself and should admit to yourself that you are often feeling as though you are in a prison and it is not making you happy in many aspects of your life.

Creating a new view of what is manhood in the society you find yourself in, is one of the biggest struggles in your view of yourself right now and you should allow yourself time to really examine your relationship with your High Priest who is the other (man) waiting to be risen from his grave. Allow him to arise from his slumber and give him the strength and power he needs to awaken.

Your High Priest is the hidden part of your manhood no one tells you about. He is the man that very few men's fathers tell them about. Why is it so hard in your culture to teach a man the basic rights of his humanness and his sex?

Your relationship with your High Priest begins the moment you acknowledge to yourself that you are capable of giving to yourself your own power to create a world that will bring you back to the instinctual knowing that "you" have the power to change your definition of your current reality. Your High Priest is a man waiting for you to be ready for him to help you change your current view of your reality. Your current view of your reality is based upon a model that may not be serving you, or you wouldn't be reading this transmission. Your current view of your reality is based upon the energy, life force and truth you are capable of. Allow yourself to bring this power to your life.

You need now to really examine what part of your life that isn't working for you and release that part of yourself that is creating sabotage in your reality right now. Your current view of your reality is based upon what others have taught you to be in the world of the "man." To consider yourself in your totality is to begin now to look at what you are capable of achieving in your world. You must examine your thoughts minutely, every moment you feel you are liable to be limited by your old world.

You must not be afraid to take a stand and to bring to your world your truth. Your truth is your barometer for your ascension and you must now look at the nature of what your truth is. As a man your truth has simplicity for you. You know the possibilities that are open to you when you act and feel truthful. Your truth comes from a place deep within yourself. You can locate it deep within your heart.

Your truth is an important barometer for your identity right now, as you are shaping your destiny around this truth.

Unveiling your truth opens up a channel and avenue for your own powerful masculine to emerge. You will begin to truthfully connect in all of life when you vibrate at a frequency, which expresses this truth. When you begin to vibrate at this frequency you will allow yourself ascension and other truth-seekers follow your energy.

You become magnetic when you are a truth-seeker. You are a magnetic energetic presence. There is a raw power around you, which magnetizes others to you and draws them to your aura. You will begin to manifest a new reality and this reality will change the cellular memory, re-coding it to accept other more powerful frequencies to you. You actually become a man to yourself and the man you become is the real essence of your manhood. Your real manhood is emerging, you are radiating and allowing. Your vibration will keep shifting like a notch on a belt. Look at your belt buckle, tighten the notch, you feel different. The tightness in the belt buckle gives you a different "feel"; it must be a feeling, a knowing that you are able to really bring to your world your newly defined masculine.

Begin now to really examine your life for flaws, for those minute little distractions which take you away from the truth that is beginning to emerge in your life right no. Just begin to really emerge from your cocoon of illusion for you are living in the world of illusion when you do not acknowledge to yourself this energy and presence which is your truth.

You are now capable of giving this to yourself. Give it to yourself now and allow yourself this new portal. This new portal is a gateway and will bring to you freedom for this is what you crave, freedom to give yourself back to yourself!

Right now you need to consider all aspects of your life and know you are truly living. You need to begin to track yourself through your whole life, and see where the pattern of masculine enslavement to your external reality really is. Your external reality projects back to you its need to control the landscape of your whole identity. Men are very easily manipulated this way. They find it difficult to really examine why they have chosen a particular identity. Men are very easily shaped by their career choice, their first choice in determining how they will perform in their world. Try and feel energetically: What was your motivation in choosing your career path? You will find if you are in resonance with your truth you will allow yourself to explore minutely the timing, when you really decided for yourself what your higher self wanted, or what your ego or subconscious created for you based upon your view matching with the carrot dangled at you by the false illusion your society created for you.

Take for example your politicians, who are predominately male, sometimes female if they conform to the stereotype. Generally when a man was choosing his career he may not have had intentionally the thought that he would have to become a victim of another reality imposed on him in his desire to create a better reality for his society. No, he probably thought, *"I am able to make a difference to my society!"* However he finds he is trapped like a bird in a cage. Once he is inside and tasted the honey-soaked cookies he has to make a decision. This is not right, this is corrupt. I must seek my truth and I must release myself to claim my authority over my small self. My desires and my ego, keep telling me this is how it is. Your society continually feeds to you this false view of reality and traps them like it does women and helpless little children.

Men become easily corrupted when they buy this version of their reality and your current state of politics reflects the barrier to real truth being presented to people who only want to live simple lives. The essence of The High Priest is to be aware and monitor his own thoughts all the time against the reality that is being presented to him. He must examine himself rigorously and always stay truthful to a part of himself that needs his truth for the survival of his totality. To become acquainted with The High Priest you must now begin to really examine your previously held beliefs and attitudes to all of life as it is presented to you. There is a need to say "yes" to the part of you that knows to be a High Priest requires valor and faith in all of life. The reality must be tested. The inner reality, as opposed to the outer or external reality must now be examined.

The inner reality begins with the self. You must just allow this self-trust to grow. There is an important aspect of The High Priest that must never be overlooked; this is his valor and trust in his valor. This word is an important one for The High Priest and it must really become part of the essence of the Priest. The Priest's essence is valor. The essence of valor is trust that the Priest will fight hard for this vibration. Meditate on the word VALOR. The Priest must strive for valor above all else. He must code his cellular memory for valor.

"I create with Valor."

Carmel: *What is "valor" exactly?*

The High Priest: Valor is the desire to fight for something that is intrinsically good. The intrinsically good something is the ideal of something. Valor is the fight for this "goodness." A High Priest has strength to fight and fight hard for valor because he knows there is no other way for him to behave. There is no other way. The beauty of valor is that it makes a man brave. A brave man is a warrior for truth and he needs to monitor this part of himself that is afraid to be truthful, firstly to himself and then to those he must serve. For he is serving one master and one master only. He must create a space of truth for himself, so he can do this. It is a brave and truthful man who can do this.

A man must want to do this with all his heart. He must fight for his heart, his true heart over his emotional heart. His emotional heart must be sacrificed for his true heart. The heart of The High Priest is the "Heart of Truth." He must access his truthful heart over his emotional heart. Find the true heart. Release the emotional heart to find the true heart.

The heart of a man is the greatest weapon for truth. He must fight for his true heart, not his emotional heart, for whom he is a slave to. Let his true heart be brave and strong so he can achieve victory over his emotional heart. Strength, courage and power are his weapons over his fears, his little selfish "boy" self that wants nothing more than getting desire satisfied.

The creating of the heart is the greatest weapon of ascension. He needs to come to a space of pure love for his truth. He must control the small ego continuously and rigorously and begin to give himself this truth continuously. There is a need now to reinforce his belief in his truth to give him all he needs as his is a truth-seeker and order creator.

Truth and order are his creations. Truth and order are needed now for him to create with in all of life. The essence of his truth must be in the availability to create. For it is through the creation process that he can find mastery over the little self.

"You" are a very important tool for creation.

The Priest is vulnerable as a man when he hasn't had this creation sharpened.

Always create with the weapon of truth.

Always create with the weapon of fire.

The Priest is a firewalker.

Firewalker Visualization Exercise:

Try and visualize yourself now as a firewalker. Really imagine the level of concentration and energy you would need for the red hot coals not to burn your soles of your feet. Feel the essence of fire searing the skin, but not burning it. The weapon of fire must be mastered for the Priest.

"I master fear through fire."
"I master fear through the element of fire."
"All fear around fire and burning must go."

Fire purges, cleanses and makes new. We burn off our old dross daily, and we create new. The essence of fire is in cleansing, cleanse and burn of the old to make new again. You need to feel the frequency of fire around you to cleanse and burn off dross. You need now to create with the essence of fire. You need strong pure energy to transform your heart. The essence of fire is

in you now to cleanse and burn off all that is not required for your journey with The High Priest. The High Priest will be born through the vibration of fire. The fire is the surrender to the Priesthood and Priests in ancient times had their initiations by fire. Fire now is allowed to be part of your cellular memory as a purging, burning vibration.

See yourself now descending into a fiery furnace. You see yourself now observing yourself, about to be consumed. Look at yourself as you lay on your coffin or stone table. Really examine yourself. You are now going to allow yourself the gift of rebirth through the element of fire. Fire is the first element of ascension. You must now feel the fire. Surrender to its mighty force and majesty to burn off all your fears and limitations about your immortal self. You are about to blow yourself apart with the heat of the flames, which will explode through your body now, cracking your skull. Feel your skull crack wide open now, as the forces rip through you, as you lay there charred and now, ash. You see your Immortal Priest begin to be born.

Watch him slowly appear now. Watch him come to life through the ashes of your past. Feel him emerging through a coil of gentle smoke or mist. Feel this now. Observe him. What has he to say to you now? What has he to bring you? Watch for him. Breathe him into you as you feel him pulsing in your root chakra. Feel him rising through your energy centers. Hold him now at your heart center. Hold him now.

Make a contract with him.
Give him your honor.
Give him your truth.
Give him your belief in what you are worth.

You will now feel his power rip into your very being. You are not afraid of each other now. You are both fearless. You are both free. You are born free. You are born free now to begin to create with your High Priest as you now are consecrated. You have consecrated yourself to him and you are now in a position to really allow him to merge with you.

Merging with your High Priest is a sacred moment, because you now have access to raw primal power of the Ancient Priesthood. In this moment of truth you and your High Priest are fused and become one. You are the essence of the sacred Priesthood and you will begin to ignite new possibilities into your life. Your life is ignited with new ideas as you have burnt off all your old fears and limitations about yourself.

Firstly you need now to create a space for your new High Priest in your life. Creating a space is a very important admission that you are ready to create with your High Priest. Your High Priest needs a consecrated space. Your High Priest is now going to develop a relationship with you like a friend only much more powerful than any human friend could because he comes from a time and space beyond humanness.

This visualization exercise will help you create a Sacred Space for your High Priest Exercise:

Begin with some breath exercises to relax you.

Imagine now, your High Priest at your front door, ready to enter your life. So what do you do now? Just allow yourself to find a consecrated space in your home. It could be a small altar dedicated to him, honoring the four sacred elements with a Tibetan bell, or any sacred object, one you feel your most spiritually connected to, or purchased in a sacred and consecrated space.

Your High Priest will need to see a space set aside to honor him daily. He will be then able to create with you, through the vibration you have created with him. This way you are respecting a part of yourself that knows this already. Your High Priest is a messenger. He is your first contact or connection with energies you will be able to create with later in your evolution. So it is very important that you make and maintain this link.

Ten minutes a day in a small ritual keeps this link. You can develop your sacred consecrated space in a private space of your home, a bedroom, study, where you can be alone and undisturbed for your 10-minute ritual to your High Priest.

Intent creates ritual. Intent to create is half the ritual itself. Intone to yourself: *"This is my sacred space with my High Priest alone and undisturbed."*

The practice of breath, purification through a bath or shower adds to the intent and settles the runaway mind. Incense to honor the air element can be used or a feather. Whatever is applicable, and easy to create your ritual with your High Priest, will be perfect.

A modern High Priest is a spiritual warrior seeking truth and creating it in his own life. You are now allowing the spirit of The High Priest to manifest a new reality for you. In manifesting a new reality, you are creating with a part of yourself that needs opening up. You are now going to get your High Priest to work with you to improve your life.

You have established your ritual for 10 minutes daily. Now you have done this you can now begin to create magic with your High Priest. Magic is the essence of trust and surrender to forces outside yourself to give you all you want for your higher good or soul's path.

Be very aware of what you wish to manifest. Let's really rip out illusions about yourself here. Cars, women, sex. Let go of your attachment to things like this, which will keep you earthbound on the karmic wheel. You must really respect your heart for true magic to happen and appear.

A true High Priest is a ceremonial magician and Shaman in other cultures. You need now to respect your spiritual mentor here, knowing he has made himself available in spirit form to manifest with you.

You are allowed to create with your High Priest in many ways. To do this you are required to really push yourself to the limits in your physical body. A man to really enact and create with his masculine has no fear of strengthening and powering his physical body. A well-toned and muscled physical body is the mark of a High Priest. The Priest really performs through the physical and the physical is a strong reminder of the Priest's connection with a man.

Allow yourself the pleasure of endurance and strengthening to increase, knowing it serves the purpose of providing The High Priest a space to grow through you. A man must work on feeling the elements. For example really hard climbing, surfing, vigorous outdoor activities, all serve to make a man proud of his masculine physique to bring his hormonal levels into resonance with his heart chakra, activating his mitochondrial DNA for "the force" to be with him.

He must feel his muscles and heart grow strong. He must strengthen his heart with rituals, which give him vigor and power. He is in this strong magnetic frequency when he allows himself the full component of his physical self, for this is where his masculine power is. His Priest creates through this energy. His Priest cannot create properly without it.

The High Priest brings truth through right action. Right action—right through your body on the right side The High Priest brings this action. He is trying to begin to allow you to explore right action in relationships. Say to yourself:

"Is this right? Does this feel right?"

The right side of your body is the portal now for right action to take place.

I bring right action through being right.

I am right.

Right now my body is balanced on the right and left sides.

Truth cannot be enacted for The High Priest until the right side of the body is aligned. Do this now:

The right side of my body is now being aligned for right action to take place.

The right hand must now rest on your heart chakra. Feel now the heart chakra opening to bring right action into every situation. Mr. Right. Here comes Mr. Right because The High Priest is Mr. Right now in your life now. Now pretend you are about to shake hands with Mr. Right. Naturally your right hand extends to meet him. Feel him now. Shake his hand. Greet him; place your hand now back at your heart. The hand is an extension of your heart and is a traditional greeting in friendship and respect. For this is what you are doing now. You are offering yourself as your gift to your High Priest. Feel him rest on your heart now as you place your hands on your heart.

You must feel the heart pumping, pouring out dross accumulated from lifetimes of fear and subjugation in relationships. Lift this load. Visualizing a dump master scooping out the deeply buried rubble of old, long-forgotten pain. Imagine you are going into your heart and you really are feeling this rubble being removed. Release it and spread the topsoil of pure love soil. Feel now the rich texture of the topsoil taking you into warmth and growth in your heart center. Feel this now, breathe this in now and create with it now.

Plant some flowers in this rich nourishing topsoil. Choose your plants, see them flourishing in the balanced elements of your heart. The heart responds to this nourishing plant. The plant responds to the heart so heart and plant become one.

Your heart is an intelligent organ, all it wants is love. For it to give love, it must receive warmth and nourishment. By choosing your plant now, planting it in your heart center you will now be able to grow your heart to receive your High Priest's love. Your High Priest's love is like a flower. It lives on love and it creates through love. You are love and your love of yourself brings your High Priest to you.

The High Priest embodies truth. For truthfulness is above all else. To be truthful is the greatest gift you can give yourself and your High Priest the chosen one by the Goddess herself, creates more and more with you through truthful action.

Carmel: *What is "truth" exactly? What do we mean by being "truthful?"*

The High Priest: We are truthful when we become truthful to the part of ourselves that has cheated the heart. We cheat our heart when we are not truthful. Imagine your plant at your heart now. It is just about to flower, you have watered it and tended to it lovingly, now just imagine that you see someone, a thief, who has watched you, silently, cunningly creep into your heart and cut the flowers off your plant. When you are not truthful your High Priest — your flower — is unable to bloom and show you the result of your hard work on yourself.

Now breathe deeply, powerfully, rhythmically and bring to you The High Priest in his full glory, his perfect masculine form now to confront the thief who wants to see your truthful heart destroyed. Feel this now. Your High Priest has appeared to you in his full powerful masculine energy. Feel him now at the right side of your heart center destroying the illusion, the fear of betrayal of the self to the self. Feel that now. He becomes now your avenger; he avenges others who are against you.

CHAPTER 3

Ptah, The Ancient Egyptian God

I asked for further guidance and assistance in helping me integrate my understanding of this process and attuned to Ptah (Ancient Egyptian God) to further support this process men must go through in creating with the balanced masculine.

Ptah Speaks: You are finding strength and power with your newly emerging masculine self now. You must begin plans for your life. You must draw up your foundations.

What are they? Who are they? Look now at your construction, your physical self; look at what you must do to construct your new physical self.

You must build your foundations through your body. What do you have to dig out of your life?

Breathe carefully, rhythmically and powerfully asking yourself:
"What do I have to uproot in my physical self?"

Dig up the roots of your old attitudes.

Look at these old attitudes as tree roots which have their source deep in your thinking. Find where the roots are now. You must dig and dig.

Do this now.

Take as long as you need. Pull up the tree roots which stop your physical self from being abused (e.g. family roots, cultural assumptions about your masculine identity, etc.) and ask yourself:

"Where do they spring from? Where do these roots have their source?"

Rip them out now. Your family tree is gone. The roots are being ripped up now. You cannot look after your physical self while you are carrying others expectations of you. You cannot bring in the feminine (the self nurturing aspect of yourself) until you have a strong foundation. Your body must be strong for your life; it's like bringing your new "bride" home to a houseful of people who want your attention. Your new "bride" (i.e. your new "self") is wanting your time and love.

Imagine now you are bringing home your "bride." She is coming to my new home; it is my physical self.

"What does she see?"

She sees my old patterns, my abuse and enslavement to other's expectations of me, and she leaves, she flies away, she is gone.

Your life now must be a foundation for your truth. Look at the structure. Look at the structure of the body. What is it saying to you? Look at where your body is most vulnerable. Feel where your body is most vulnerable now. Breathe love into that part of your body and feel your High Priest constructing new limbs or body parts. Go into the machinery of the body; arm, shoulders etc. Visualize yourself through an x-ray machine, taking photos looking at where the problems are. See those problems now.

Go to the bones; find the problem you need to fix. Look at the problem like a builder.

"What am I going to do to fix this? What help do I need to fix this?"

Now you must go back to the source. Where did the problem come from? Feel where the problem could have come from. Track its source. My shoulders ache. Track the problem. Do they carry too many heavy loads? Carry lighter loads, both physically and emotionally. Your body is the barometer of your power to really enact the creative masculine.

By attuning to Ptah, the Ancient Egyptian God who creates through order and structure, your life will become one of order and structure. You are now your foundation builder.

This exercise will help you create a new reality.
Construct a square:

What is your square made of? Metal, bricks, etc. Make your construction strong and truthful. Don't give yourself inferior products. Look at the food you eat. Look at your exercise program. You must now construct your body as a temple. Your body becomes the structure for you to build your new life. You need now to perform the miracle of seeing your body as a perfect structure with no flaws, no compromises. You deserve this. Feel this now!

Your High Priest is a channel for you to embrace the masculine because the source of the energy is purely a creative one and in that respect the creative force of the masculine becomes enacted in a creative way. You must seek to surrender to the creative masculine in your daily activities. Your creative masculine is focused goal-directed activity. It involves concentration and action. It embraces the balance in this creative action. It is not aggressive, and doesn't assume authority over others or misuse authority over oneself.

To embrace your masculine self in the creative aspect is to find resonance with your High Priest first and allow "his" masculine energy to channel through you. By being aware of him in you, you will be directed to explore the creative masculine energy needed for you to create momentum and life force for your truth.

Your creativity will become more focused and goal directed and will be able to create outcomes, which will get results in your life fast. To embrace and surrender to the creative masculine is to find within oneself a respect for the source of all life. To respect the source of all life is a respect for yourself within.

"I am a creative masculine being having an experience in my humanness right now."

My humanness is not a linear experience (like a line). It is experiential and can be experienced through different aspects of myself at any given moment. By being attuned to your High Priest you will be allowing yourself to embrace the creative masculine principle of selfhood.

When the self is engaged, the masculine becomes activated automatically. Being aware of this will create resonance with all of life. All of life is then at the ready, because you have been attuned to the masculine. By now you will have realized we are on the journey to the heart so when the heart is engaged, the self emerges and the masculine principle is automatically activated.

It is the task of the journeyer (you) to follow this road to the heart. Your sole task in your humanness is to get to the heart. It doesn't matter how many incarnations you take but you will continue to need to experience humanness until you reach this point. The High Priest is a vital link for this journey, because you cannot get to the Heart Chakra, without the masculine being acknowledged, i.e.

"I need this to grow."
"I need to acknowledge the masculine principle to grow my inner masculine."

Ask yourself:
"Who symbolizes for me the balanced creative heart-centered drive in the true masculine form?"

Is it a fictional character or a character in a film? Is it a loved family member, who would, in your consciousness, embody these principles?

We all need a masculine hero who embodies the true essence of human manhood. Go back to your childhood. Who were the fictional male characters? Breathe deeply and begin to go back to your father, grandfather or other male figures in your family lineage. Our biological lineage carries the blueprint for how we create and manifest through the masculine. Our ancestors will be very important in creating The High Priest within you.

You must draw on the positive attributes of family members of your lineage, from both your mother's and father's side. Ancient bloodlines are vital links to draw upon as the cellular memory can be activated to bring forth the positive masculine principle.

This following meditation exercise will help you identify your masculine and feminine energies and how they can be balanced through The High Priest.

Breathe deeply, powerfully and rhythmically establishing a link with your "Higher Self" and heart's intelligence. Through a mirror, look at the left side of your face with a clean sheet of paper covering the right side of your face. Draw an imaginary line right down the middle of your face.

Through the left side you will begin to observe the feminine ancestry, on your mother's side. The strengths and weaknesses can be noted and integrated. The masculine side, (the right side of the face) alternatively reveals an untapped source of power and masculine energy through your father's masculine lineage. By just observing the differences between the left and right sides of your face, you can begin to gain access to the secrets of your face and the journey inward reveals itself. Your High Priest will be waiting to reveal himself and bring you into alignment with your truth.

Your character is revealed in the shape and structure of your face. This "face" faces the world and shows the "outer world" your "inner self." By being in alignment with your High Priest you are re-awakening the potential, which lay inside you, opening and revealing itself to your outer world.

Opening your eyes to your potential, through your High Priest, will bring you totally into a new vibration and your first challenge will be to identify your High Priest speaking through you.

Imagine a scene where you, as a man or woman, wanting to attune to the vibration of The High Priest and now finding the Priest (like a guide beside you) giving you instructions for acting and behaving in a certain way.

After I was attuned to my High Priest, the very next day, I was challenged by a man who with his own sense of superiority and seniority told me point blank how he was an authority on a particular subject. He was condescending and rude. My "old" self would have challenged his arguments. However, I felt myself change direction. I stopped and just said nothing. I could feel the presence of something guiding me, and I perceived it to be my High Priest. In changing my response, the man could see that he was alone with his own need to intellectually control an outcome in a conversation. I felt the shift in him and he drifted off. The energy of The High Priest gave me the feeling of inner power over the man's need to control my responses.

Embodying The Divine Masculine of All Truth, Through The High Priest

We are all in the perfect space to create a deep and meaningful relationship with our own inner masculine. For this is what The High Priest brings, the need to fully develop and connect to your own inner masculine. Strength and power comes and a true sense of belonging to a part of yourself that has been split off or disconnected from your soul self.

Having The High Priest in your totality is strengthening you for battle; the battle being with the part of you that doesn't want the invigorating aspect of battle. Battle is the word the Priest uses to help you grow your inner masculine. Aligning yourself now to this energy, brings you into alignment with the word "battle" as not being a negative thing but an invigorating power being unleashed within you to create strength and power to slay the parts of yourself that won't respond to your need to want to win, to conquer and defeat.

By being in a state of surrender allows your unconscious to be made available to you to begin the journey inward to claim your authority over the part of yourself that will not conform to the idea of having your masculine fully encoded in you.

You must remember that most empowered people have either consciously or unconsciously come to terms with their inner masculine and embraced it as part of their totality. The challenge for humans in ascension is the belief that they can come to a space of acceptance of this part of themselves that lies dormant within them.

You are not alone when you explore this mystery. The mystery of The High Priest is to accept and create with all aspects of forgiving the self and creating with the self that will resist the challenge to change. The High Priest's role in contemporary life for the understanding of the masculine is to really explore why you need this power and how you will use the power.

It's very easy to be a victim of your own enslavement in fear of the masculine. You must now allow strength to code to you and bring the positive in and allow the true trust process to enfold and create with you. You are love when you allow this process to take place because the masculine will bring the balance and much-needed truth to your world. It is your responsibility once you have decided to allow the forces of the masculine to begin to carve power and trust into your psyche.

The essence of the masculine lies in trusting the masculine force to work for you not against you. The essence of the masculine is in the honoring of the natural forces through the masculine progress. For example, man has always seen it as his role to conquer and rise above the natural forces to destroy them and rule them. Look at your world and the conditions you are all living in. You see yourself living in a world "man" has made through working the wrong way with the natural forces. The world of technology, which is "man made," can create a barrier toward the truth of an ascending masculine soul. Alternatively, nature must be respected by the masculine forces, which will kill man in the end, if not respected. Man who works through the unbalanced masculine creates fear and alienation from his planet and his world. He must seek to redress this within himself.

All those who work against the natural masculine force which is to work with nature, destroy a part of themselves. They destroy their own creative masculine force. They are ripping out a part of themselves they need to grow and this is where the problem is, because men do not even understand their own inner masculine. It is their own inner masculine they are destroying when they do not allow the essence of their true masculine self to create with nature, not rebel against the primal forces of nature, which give the masculine principal its strength and vigor.

To do your daily tasks, which appear mundane or repetitive with love and surrender to your truth brings the vibration of The High Priest closer to you. Service to the Priesthood is the most important thing you must try and achieve right now, as you delve into the mystery of the power of the Priesthood. Exulting truth through the masculine principle is the essence of The High Priest and for this journey you must take within yourself. You create an opening or vortex within your own cellular memory to go and allow the essence of the Priesthood to come with you to create together.

It's like getting into a car with a stranger. Imagine now, you are on the side of a long silent road; you don't know what to do. This is an exercise only and does not imply that anyone walking on silent roads alone need to expose themselves to unnecessary dangers. A car pulls up beside you and the unknown man invites you on this journey with him. You will need to find a space within yourself to trust this man because you have invited yourself to participate in the adventure of the Priesthood. You must now trust the part of yourself that wanted the experience and now that part of yourself needs the experience as well. You must reinforce your trust in yourself and know that you are going to bring to your world a knowing that you are ready to go beyond a part of yourself that is surrendering, not struggling to this masculine force growing inside you.

By evoking the spirit of the masculine in your daily ritual you are calling home a lost part of yourself. The essence of your truth is to find the missing bits of your lost masculine. This is essential for humans to understand. It is very difficult to grow without the perfect seed. Imagine a tree strong and powerful and protective. The strong, protective tree must begin with a seed. The seed must be of the best quality. Certified seeds make the best crops. So it is with you. You must have the best seed to plant when you find yourself confronted with any difficulty, which sees you, de-powered and non-productive. Strong, powerful tree = strong, powerful seed. You are allowing this seed to grow strong and powerful when you evoke the masculine principle. You do not need any one to provide that support for you. It's very important that you face this and realize this truth. You need to really provide a space in your life now to recognize that the tree must have strong seeds for it to grow.

The balanced masculine/feminine within all humans must be made strong and whole.

Reflect now on strong, powerful, protective people in your life. When you look at their lives, you will witness that their masculine is operating, and they are not afraid of it.

To be able to have the freedom to go anywhere anytime brings a feeling of power. Imagine now, going anywhere in the world or another galaxy even the moon. Would you go on a mystery tour bus? If the tour bus came to your front door and said, *"Here I am, I can take you anywhere any time, enjoy!"*

Meditate now, on where you would go. Would you want to leave home at all? Would you travel in your own country or another part of the world or another planet or civilization? Would you go down to the center of the Earth?

This little exercise will begin to allow you to explore your world with The High Priest. The masculine frequency is one of protection, order and freedom. Allow yourself to explore where you would go, the energy belts in our energetic structure correspond to our view of our self.

Now if you want to stay at home, you are still operating from the base chakra, which needs the security of your home. Your desire center in the belly center relates to your emotional/ego wishes. Your heart center brings yourself into the picture, i.e. where does your heart want to go?

Taking your soul on a holiday brings you further home (i.e. out of this world). This exercise shows how your High Priest is growing in you, and how you perceive your world. For example, if you want to explore other galaxies, the moon, stars, your star home, your soul is expanding your conscious view of reality. If you decide to explore the inside of the Earth herself, you are honoring the source of your human incarnation.

The confidence in your masculine grows daily when you ritualistically honor The High Priest inside you. Both The High Priest and High Priestess growing inside us bring the completeness to our base chakra. We cannot ascend if the base chakra is not fully earthed and rock solid.

Embodying The Divine Masculine of All Truth, Through The High Priest

The High Priest is a fundamental pillar in the ascension process as you are strengthening and aligning yourself to the true earth. It is only if we are earthed can we then fly. The High Priest will change your consciousness to believe in the true masculine process. This masculine process cannot grow when you are in a de-powered space at any time. Strengthening your body, mind and soul by truly believing in the power of your High Priest brings to you all the requirements for ascension. Your training must be ongoing and you must continually monitor your reactions to the active, balanced masculine within you. It is the greatest gift you can give yourself, whether male or female, as the foundations must be kept perfectly strong every day. If not the rest of your hard work on your ascension is just eroded. It cannot hold itself.

Man or woman, it doesn't matter really who you are as long as you are observing the imbalances in your psyche and seek to address them. You are helping to rescue yourself from your enslavement to bring truth and knowledge of the self. The High Priest has the key to this mystery, as he is one of the missing parts of your own jigsaw puzzle in your humanness. He is one of the most important triggers for your humanness because the essence of your own masculine is encoded in your cells and must be brought out. You need to feel the power and essence of all life to create with you and allow you the privilege of access to your High Priest. You must feel the essence of truth and oneness in all of life and live it and create with it. The Priest's message is one of truth for ascension. Your relationship with your High Priest is your own missing link to your divine creation, yourself. You are now in a position to bring this creation into focus through attention to detail in every living thing. Your High Priest is you, all parts of you belong to your High Priest because the masculine principle acknowledged and balance brings you into alignment with your truth.

You need to recognize the power of the masculine to create with you and you need to recognize the immortals living with you when you honor the creative energies of the masculine.

Your immortal self can only express itself by your observance of yourself and you are reminding yourself continually of who you are really and what you are capable of for your life right now. You are processing the process of observing emotions through the vibration of the masculine. The masculine vibration is enacted whenever you are bringing to your world your capacity to know yourself through love and peace.

The High Priest is such a figure. This figure fills out all the blemishes in your landscape where you have been betrayed by the masculine process. The masculine process betrays continually in your society because of the misuse of the masculine principle by men and women in power. This creates a distrust of the masculine principle. Look at all the wars in your world right now; look at the wars in your country, your state, city, village. Is this not a misuse of the masculine principle? You would see the parallel of misuse of the masculine principle in the way women and children are treated in your world generally, you would see this misuse in every aspect of your culture which destroys the trust between healthy balance between men and women.

Your worldview must change, you must not allow yourself to be enslaved by the masculine principle which seeks to destroy and not create. By bringing into alignment your own inner masculine you are going beyond your previously held belief of the destructive force of the masculine principle.

Allowing yourself to be aware of every little thing that causes a block in your view of yourself brings you to a point where you can begin to remember your power through the masculine process. For example, you need to feel that you are fully capable of enacting the masculine principal through The High Priest in everything that you do.

Say and feel: *"The essence of who I am is in this principle and it reveals itself in many ways."* You, for example, act out a scenario in your life where the masculine principle is needed (i.e. You are attending an important business meeting, a contract to be signed or anything which requires the masculine principle to be working for you.)

You need to see the situation as having a fruitful and pleasant outcome, pleasing to you both and everyone being happy. You must now feel your High Priest beside you even talking or not talking in some cases. You need to really believe in your ability to give to yourself all the outcome requires with the Priest present.

This exercise can be acted out before any encounter with anyone where the masculine principle needs to be evoked. You are free to create with the masculine in all that you do say and feel in any encounter where there is a need to enact the masculine principle.

Create the scene in your mind having a happy outcome and release — surrender to the force of the masculine through The High Priest. Discovering the power of your masculine brings to your world new power. Your power radiates out and you become one with the forces of light which merge with you.

Your surrendering to The High Priest is always a challenge and you need to remember you must create a little ritual for your High Priest to become active in your cellular memory. For example, you must just allow the principle of love to surround you for when you love yourself you can find your relationship with yourself strengthened enough to bring the Priests power to you through the masculine principle.

You are now going to establish a ritual space to begin your devotions to your High Priest. You begin by allowing yourself the gift of your High Priest to create with you in the enactment of devotion. Devotions create order and presence of love for your own inner masculine. Your own inner masculine must be honored every day through a ritual to your High Priest. You must feel yourself unfolding everyday to this aspect of yourself. You are one in truth with yourself when you do this. The message of love is in the enactment of ritual. You are free to explore your relationship with your High Priest this way. Create a space where ritual and devotion can be done daily, for your creative masculine to be evoked.

Your love for yourself must be above all considerations when you embark on such a challenging and intimate discovery of yourself as a High Priest. This is a new way of looking at your humanness and you must feel that you are ready for the many old emotions which surface. Making time for this inner exploration will bring to you a source of richness you cannot possibly imagine. You will begin to go and find that part of yourself which has been lost and now needs finding. For you to find your own masculine is to really open up your world to potential you could never imagine. Your High Priest is like your own gold miner, encouraging you to find the gold mine in the underground tunnel of our life.

Look at yourself now, standing at the entrance to the tunnel in the desert landscape in a remote place, away from civilization. Your High Priest is the miner, and he knows where the golden treasures are. He invites you to join him in this adventure; this adventure is now to begin. You know the risks, the perils, the dangers. Your body has been prepared, you know what you want to find. For you will not want to go further or even begin until you know what the rewards will bring you. List the rewards of the golden casket, opening to reveal the treasures of gold and precious gems and metals.

For you now it is important to list the things you want from your masculine for this is where the masculine is. You must now just feel the masculine in your life and live it imaginatively so you can begin to explore what you want from your journey. You must want the rewards, before you begin the journey. To begin the journey and not know or challenge yourself to receive the reward is only punishing yourself. It's a form of mental cruelty to your own inner child. Imagine saying to a child, "We are going on a hazardous journey, it will be dark and sometimes very fearful. I do not know if we will survive, but I better go." Your child self hears this and becomes dismayed.

"Why?" he/she asks "Why? Why?"

Now you must examine very carefully what you want from your inner exploration to find the golden treasure, your High Priest masculine self.

Feel and engage with every single atom in your being what connecting to and receiving from The High Priest will bring you. List at least five different attributes the powerful frequencies will bring you, so you will stay disciplined and focused for the journey ahead.

Now if you want to re-cap lets go through The High Priest's attributes for your life.

CHAPTER 4

Attuning to The High Priest

By reading this transmission you will be attuned spontaneously to The High Priest. You may experience shifts in energy, tiredness or cranky feelings. Enormous resistances emerge, as the cellular memory is being re-coded for remembering your true masculine power. Your own energetic matrix is being re-coded. Expect shifts in energy, like power surges, tingling hands and feet. I was beginning to perceive at this point that the information coming through was gender inclusive, and women were being invited to be attuned to The High Priest frequency energetically.

The material was constantly being tested in my healing center with clients.

My student wanted the initiation, to further empower herself. She is a successful businesswoman in the real estate industry. Here is what The High Priest channeled, when she began her initiation ceremony.

"You will feel what balanced masculine power is. You need this as your masculine is not allowing you the full expression of your feminine. You must now remember that The High Priest brings truth between men and women and your new High Priest will stop the fear you have around men, especially where you wish to control them."

Beginning such a relationship is like having an adopted child. You are seeking the company, the joy of giving and receiving, of being part of something, part of you but new to you as well. Your adopted child is very vulnerable to the pressures you place on him/her; so don't be in a hurry to make "things" happen all at once. You must just feel your way with the new energies of The High Priest. It is an entirely different feeling and one you will get used to in time. Be very gentle with this aspect of yourself that needs nurturing for you need to really feel the power and essence of yourself growing in response to the call of The High Priest.

Tony, another student, requested initiation; he reported that The High Priest felt to him like a male friend he could relate to intimately. Tony felt he needed the masculine because his father wasn't there for him especially in his adolescent years (his mother even had to teach him how to shave). This absence created a void in his life and he sought the company of male friends to relate to intimately. This wasn't proving satisfactory either, he felt de-powered and afraid most of the time.

Through his High Priest initiation and inner exploratory work with his masculine he has developed groundedness and a quiet confidence, which is making him more comfortable in the expression of his sexuality and career. His heart has opened and he has forgiven much of his painful past. He is now looking forward to being able to allow himself growth in his career path and deeper, more meaningful relationships.

Always the pressure for a human is the loss that accompanies the new relationship. There is power, much power in creating with your High Priest, but the problem will be in letting go. The celebration of your new friend brings excitement; it's rather like getting engaged or celebrating a graduation.

The excitement becomes apparent to those around you. Your heart chakra is opening. You are feeling good.

The problem begins now. What are you going to do with those you leave behind? You must be careful here, because The High Priest challenges all previously held definitions of yourself. You must be very kind with the people you must let go and release them gently. You must acknowledge to yourself that many of the supports, the crutches you have had have only been there because of your vulnerability. You felt isolated and lost and many people filled this void.

Now the world is filling up with your newly emerging masculine. Your newly emerging masculine now allows you to really create in a space of purity for what you are and who you are. You are one in essence with all of life when you begin your journey with your masculine for he guides the road and brings you home to yourself. You must acknowledge to yourself.

I am on my way home.
I am on my own.
I am safe and free in the exploration of my masculine self.
I am loved.

Allowing the masculine spirit to emerge requires dedication to your own soul's purpose. You are ready when you allow yourself the belief in the ascension process. You wouldn't bother otherwise. The training is an inner alchemy, an inner truth coming to you. You must feel the commitment to not only yourself in your disciplines or practices but to all of life. For all of life partakes in the journey of The High Priest.

"Ra" first appeared to me when I began my training under the Egyptian Seichim-Sekhem Reiki frequency. My early morning pool meditations began by evoking the energy and power of the Sun God — Atum Ra. Bringing Ra into my consciousness enabled me to begin my own inner journey with the masculine for the first time, bringing strength and courage to fight; and the will to keep going in a personally tumultuous relationship.

The High Priest's vibration brings raw transformative masculine power to fight for your soul. Your soul is the only thing you must fight for in life and your truth now becomes evident to you, (and in my case) for the first time in a pure clear form. Bringing the power of the masculine in destroys the patriarchal system. It's like lifting off layer upon layer of cruelty and hatred to all people who try and allow new souls freedom to explore their totality. This is a very powerful process, because you are just acknowledging your reality doesn't have to be there. You need to really examine your external reality created through the masculine process and bring to your world your view of your own inner masculine which does not have to use this model, which controls and which will eventually destroy itself.

Your life must bring the beauty and strength of the masculine in every way imaginable. Your view of your masculine does not in any way conform to the external view of the patriarchal world. Your first attempt to examine the patriarchal world, the worldview of destruction and not creation comes to you in many forms and in many ways. Look carefully now at the patriarchal institutions who have forced their agendas on you. Start with your education system, teaching models, ideals and structures. Your institutions of learning parody fear and alienation. They are rigid and fixed in a narrow definition of how the human is supposed to learn. They do not allow for free expression of an inner quest for truth.

Your culture is created through learning and holding true to its essence. You must examine your learning, your schooling, your response to education and seek to remedy the gross disservice your soul has been given in your learning institutions. Your soul is raped through the mismanagement of learning.

Allowing the forces of nature to surround you will always bring you into resonance with your High Priest. The forces of nature are always your guide to a balanced and ascended life with your High Priest. You must seek to control the forces, which destroy the part of yourself that won't take responsibility for the masculine.

Embodying The Divine Masculine of All Truth, Through The High Priest

You must feel the essence of truth in the enactment of the masculine process; your truth cannot be fully realized until you take care of this vital part of your unique creation of yourself. Love, truth and oneness of the masculine allows responsibility to one's self.

In an initiation ceremony with one student, Amanda (she was 21 years old when she had her initiation to The High Priest), her High Priest revealed to her in channeling in her ceremony that

"The High Priest will grow Amanda up. She is missing the balanced masculine because of her upbringing and her inability to really have boundaries around men. She will find strength and endurance and be more observational. She will not feel she needs men for security." This is what she needed from her High Priest.

Later that month, I conducted a full moon ceremony in a sacred beach setting with five other students of the mysteries. This was an extraordinary ceremony on a partial eclipse of the full moon at dusk.

One student was a 42-year-old man. His High Priest revealed this message to him.

"David will feel the vibration of The High Priest in all areas of his life. The High Priest is there to help him accept responsibility for himself. He has never nurtured himself. He has not been able to accept the responsibility for himself first. He feels he must give to others to accept him so that he can accept himself. He has a sacred responsibility to himself first and he must use his High Priest always for his own physical self-maintenance. He must strengthen and clear his physical body from misuses and he must feel the power in his body to control and harness his emotions, which create havoc in his energy field. He needs proper disciplines and deep breathing techniques to balance the incoming channels of psychic material. This time he is being given the gift to actually create a balanced and meaningful life for himself."

These two examples bring to your awareness how The High Priest's vibration manifests itself in a woman and a man. The role of The High Priest is actually gender inclusive. You must feel the power of allowing The High Priest's presence in the two examples. It is very important to feel The High Priest really being part of your consciousness now as you have come far enough in reading this channeled material to begin to find your own relationship with the forces that shape this representation of your own identity.

Your life force will begin to change and you will not feel so needy in encounters with people of both sexes. You will feel the power of your truth emerge with the power of The High Priest's role in your life; you must remember that when you create with your High Priest you are stepping outside the boundaries of your cultural and social definition of yourself. This is where your power is. Your power is in maintaining your own relationship with your inner masculine, which is your birth right. Your force of Sekhem energy (or Kundalini, Shakti energy) will begin to rise like a serpent up your spine and you will experience powerful shifts in awareness. Begin to open your consciousness to this new view of yourself now. Bring now the vibration of trust for yourself in the process of these initiations. You are in the presence of some very powerful, illuminated beings then you channel this aspect of yourself, which lay dormant like a serpent coiled in its basket.

Visualize now your serpent power. In ancient Egypt the serpent power was called Sekhem and in India today it is called Shakti.

Let's call it:
"The Serpent Power."

Serpents create many different responses in humans from fear to fascination.

There is something magnetic about watching a snake. I want you to become familiar with the "serpent" power you have within you. Your serpent power is the combined energies of your masculine and feminine energy. With this power you will create life force and you will begin to feel the power the ancient ones had access to. Your relationship with your power determines whether you will evolve through your journey in being human. This is your power and the serpent is the symbol for this power. Allow yourself to become familiar with your serpent power by watching it. Visualize yourself now watching a serpent. Now associate the images, which come to mind. For me it is the biblical image of the serpent in the Garden of Eden, tempting Adam and Eve to eat the forbidden fruit.

Your early conditioning about serpents will determine your readiness to embrace your own inner serpent. Let's look at the image in Adam and Eve's story. The serpent tempts and they both taste the apple even though they are in paradise. Our serpent power tempts us to challenge our definition of our old world or to embrace our totality. The serpent is us. It was the energy of Adam and Eve themselves, which activated their own inner desires, represented by the serpent. By mastering their own serpent and releasing their fears about immortality (for this what they were being challenged to do) they could have integrated their own inner Shakti/Sekhem energy and evolved to being immortal.

Serpent power is your power to control the chaotic forces, which surface when you activate your own basket of fears. This can unleash some extraordinary emotional responses. These emotional responses create triggers which set off other emotional reactions. You can experience severe anxiety, sometimes even depression.

So why bother? *"Why not keep the serpent in the basket?"* It's too much to suffer; yet you know there is a part of you that must prod the serpent. Loosening the coils, which keep your emotional life contained, helps you explore your potential. If contained they cannot be explored. They must be exposed for what they are. However there is no hurry with this process, just be kind to your "inner serpent." Tell this part of yourself that you need to explore your serpent power through the balanced masculine.

Your outcome is to become the pure-hearted High Priest capable of allowing this "self" to emerge. It's rather like a baby having the consciousness to be able to see it's purely developed self in adult form. *"Wow look at me! Aren't I just so powerful with my emotions balanced?"* Your emotions are your biggest barrier to your heart center and they are your greatest power.

Evoking emotions and feeling good helps humans evolve. However the problem begins when the emotions strike back at you, like the serpent being prodded with a hot poker from its slumber and unconscious state. When you are fearful you do nothing and the serpent slumbers. However when you attack your emotions with a hot poker you find your serpent, your unconscious sleeping emotions, attack you and even kill you. Emotions out of control are an example of this. Depression, anxiety, suicidal tendencies can be your own emotions striking back at you. Your serpent power when attacked by you will retaliate. It knows no other way. It is the primitive part of you. Some people call it our "shadow" side our "dark self," attacking our evolving or love-filled self and there is a struggle. These energies take no prisoners. It is energy, which must be balanced, or it can destroy. Much of what you are seeing in our society is these energies running rampant, the dark/shadow against the light love-filled self.

For your High Priest the masculine principle being balanced is the primary task for your humanness. It is an evolving thing and must be observed. You must find your High Priest in all of your life where the masculine principle needs to be observed and understood.

Harnessing your own masculine which if not controlled destroys a balanced heart-centered life. For a man, the primary principle is one of surrender, for in surrendering to your own nature, knowing its potential to destroy your own evolvement calls for much discipline and strength. Your serpent, your own destructive nature, destroys you if not tamed with compassion and kindness to this part of yourself, which must grow.

Imagine yourself now bringing home a small boy. You don't know what he needs until he is observed. Observe your emotions; they are the trigger to your controlling the wild colt/boy. These energies are powerful and cells carry a memory, which triggers them. You must feel now that your humanness deserves such love. Love the wild untamed part of yourself. Do not accept your/its destructive side.

Now, by having your spiritual guide/mentor High Priest you are able to integrate these energies and balance them. You become an observer of yourself and in that respect you see those parts of yourself, which are acting out of control destroying the potential of your humanness.

The definition of the inner masculine is an important new energy for you to open up to. The inner masculine is open to receiving. For the masculine to be fully integrated into your energetic structure you need to embrace the vibration of receiving. You must feel the energy and essence of what it is to receive through the masculine principle. To receive through the masculine is to know that you have controlled the rampant emotions which want domination for the sake of an outlet.

The emotion is raw, powerful, penetrating. It has the capacity to destroy. It is in the process of destroying the very environment it needs to survive. In this aspect it is your own parasite, which seeks to devour yourself, your truth and your capacity to live a fully realized life.

To know this aspect of your own inner life is a challenging breakthrough in your consciousness. Awareness of where and how the "serpent" shadow will appear prepares you for the blows you will give yourself when you meet opposition. See your shadow serpent as being true to its nature. The nature of a cobra is to strike. This is its nature. Its natural weapons are its instinctual cunning and predatory nature.

Let's take an example of a family gathering. It is a birthday party or wedding. All the characters are there with their serpents in their handbags, trousers, etc. They are nicely housed and contained.

You say to yourself, *"This is going to be a challenge or a fun event."* Let's look at the characters. *"Which characters, relations, etc. at this event will demonstrate to me my raw inner exposed self?"*

Family karmas emerge as you begin to relax and have food and refreshments. You can sense the energy shift in the space. There is an "atmosphere." It is beginning to build up. The handbags are being opened. The trouser pockets reveal the "serpent." The serpent wants to come out and play. The masculine principle is one of protection. The father protects the family. He provides love, support and order. Apply this principle to your own self now.

Whose serpent has got out of the bag?

How are you going to react?

The control is loosened; vibrations of the runaway serpents start playing with each other. It's like watching boxers in a ring. *Who is going to give the first punch? How are you going to retaliate or receive the blow?* We all have been part of these family or group scenarios.

Let's look at the wedding party. The bride and groom represent balanced love, which is heart centered. Well meaning "relations and friends" seize upon the "single free" family members, asking; *"Why aren't you married? When are 'you' going to tie the knot?"*

The moment is upon you. You have been seized by a serpent. It has you by the throat. It is at that moment you decide how your serpent is going to react. You can strike back, blow for blow or you can tell your trained serpent that this is an attack and you must contain your instinctual fear, and prevent your survival mechanism from striking back.

Visualize now your trainer, your High Priest having trained the serpent for the blow. Be kind and loving to your own serpent now and just remind yourself that your High Priest, your trainer has you prepared. This is the test of self-love, self-love is to know the attack is an unconscious attack on your self-love, your High Priest is now your trainer, he whispers in your ear a message:

"To get to your High Priest you must breathe and give yourself space. This space is one of allowing the wisdom through your High Priest to filter down the layer of primitive fear the attack represents."

Virtually every hour we are attacked in such a way. For example some "serpents" are devious and cunning. They know us well. They know how to draw us out of our baskets. The people who have access to our heart are often the biggest betrayers. Loved ones, children, parents. They know our closet of fears. We have created an agenda for someone when we have an expectation of them. Our agenda for ourselves matches their agenda for us.

Our agenda for ourselves is in fact where our problem begins. By being attached to an outcome, we create barriers to our higher truth and we feel fearful when someone acts out a scenario that we ourselves have created. The film "What the Bleep do we Know" demonstrates practically every scenario family's project on to each other at an American family (of Polish background) wedding. Through the observer self, every imaginable social situation is played back to the leading character Marcia, the photographer whose fear of love and commitment in marriage see her being able to finally create through a receiving encounter with a guest.

The aspect of love we must develop to create with our High Priest is one of true trust. You must establish that this is a true trust relationship, pure with no agenda for an outcome. Developing the art of communication with The High Priest must be first established through intention. No judgments and pre-planned agendas is the key to developing a balanced loving relationship with your High Priest.

Our society creates imbalances in relationships by its very nature. Not only does it leave men marginalized to their true masculine potential but it deprives women of receiving from balanced male energy or even allowing themselves to seek a potential mating partner with a man who has the attributes of The High Priest.

Vanessa is such a client, an academic, single mother of a child whose father is a "token" carer. With a history of broken relationships, she could not manage to include a man in her life because of her fears of trusting men to help her develop confidence in expression of relationships. Her inner nature is to instantly distrust men although she is a warm, loving woman who would love a balanced relationship.

She is a committed student of the mysteries and has studied widely and taken training in the feminine goddess frequency. However there is an imbalance. She cannot trust her own inner masculine to develop a healthy life for herself. She was at this point in her soul's journey when I suggest she take The High Priest initiation.

I felt that by having a "friend" on the frequency of the masculine through The High Priest could help her create a meaningful supportive energy for her life for her heart to grow. She found in the ceremony a sense of peace with her Priest, she felt someone she could be a friend with. His message to her was:

"You need to go out into the world trusting you are able to have a friend. You are now bringing to your world this trust and love. When you create with me, you bring a friend to your world."

Les has requested to be attuned to The High Priest in The Atlantis Rising Mystery School. His wife has found with her High Priestess a new ability to discriminate and find her relationship with her feminine. Both she and Les felt by him having the initiation into The High Priest, he could find a sense of true balance in his masculine. His inner masculine has not been explored yet because he, like many men, has never been exposed to the power of his masculine energy.

"The High Priest brings to any soul the power to manifest. To be able to manifest is to realize yourself as a magician and to feel the essence of the magician inside you. The High Priest is an amazing magical frequency because he keeps you grounded in the earth to manifest. You cannot manifest unless energy and power is being made available to you and your manifestation skills will develop with love of your truth. With The High Priest you will be able to manifest to instantly give you what your Higher Self needs. Your manifestation grows magically and powerfully the power of your magical self is available for you when you create with your High Priest, because he creates with ritual and order to bring balance to your world."

It's very difficult to believe that a man cannot receive the benefits of the masculine in a culture, which honors it in sport, government and economics. The men who are creating with the masculine principle are balanced in their masculine and are not feeding off the energy of the unbalanced masculine. They are aware of how destructive it is to them, as well as to society and are able to develop discrimination in what they are supposed to experience in our world by observing their emotional reaction to the masculine expression in our society.

Chapter 5

Identify with your High Priest

Right now you may be wishing to further develop your identity with your High Priest. He now allows you to explore your identity with him.

The High Priest Speaks: Your identity now must be your first priority. To identify with what The High Priest offers in balanced heart-centered relationships begins now with the opportunity to trust in the process of all life. You are a witness to your own ability to heal and change the DNA of your sex orientation (this means you apply your sexual orientation in the world) and in doing so; you are transforming all aspects of your own identity. You must identify with only one thing, your own masculine nature and the understanding of it, to bring around deep and profound cellular change. You are opening up to new frequencies, new pathways in your identification of yourself at the cellular level. You are bringing to your life your hope that you are able to receive the peace and order, this balance offers. For this to happen you need to restructure your previously held belief about what it is to be masculine in the world you see yourself living in. Again, the need to really examine core beliefs about your identity will shape your truth.

You must challenge now what you choose to become. You become what you create. You are now creating in yourself a view of yourself that must be incorporated into your view of who you are in your totality. This view of yourself is the beginning of change in your view of truth. You need now to allow the sense of truth to become one with you in all that you seek in your life right now. The essence of all life lies in the application of truth for ascension. At the basic level you are really allowing yourself the power to bring to your life this truth. For all energy to be brought into human consciousness you are connecting to an important truth within yourself. You are opening up to the truth of absolute surrender and belief in your ability to change everything in your world. Why? Because you are redefining yourself outside your worldview, outside your definition of yourself. Your definition of yourself brings peace and stability to you when you define yourself in this way. This is the way of truth. The way of truth must come before anything else now in your view of yourself if you are to bring the sacred priest hood to your energetic view of your new reality. You are birthing yourself totally in view of all aspects of your new reality. You are love.

Your role is to always integrate the opposing forces which will take you apart. Your world is being ripped apart by the current global financial crisis the unbalanced masculine creates. The very thing "man" wants is the very thing he chooses to destroy. He destroys an aspect of himself daily when he doesn't honor the masculine forces.

By bringing the masculine forces into alignment with all life, The High Priest is re-awakened in a man. He is being re-structured into a new form; he is being crafted and brought into alignment with his truth. The energy of the masculine brings down the creative force. The actual creative force is a masculine process. The creative masculine is alchemy. Evoking this creative masculine force brings your masculine into alignment with all life. Bring to you now the force of true peace and growth. Man does not want to destroy what he has created; man himself has created this force through the utilization of his own masculine creative force. He destroys the very thing "he" has created, this is "himself." It is important that "man" identify this force within himself and stop destroying the very thing he has created within himself, his creative masculine.

Allowing your masculine to be part of your totality requires you to separate yourself from human collective consciousness of what the masculine is. You must feel that your definition of the masculine is not what the "masculine is." If you use society's model you are going to be trapped by media who primarily control the forces of the masculine and feminine identity. You are giving yourself the gift of non-identification with your culture definition of the "masculine." Your role in identifying the masculine is determined by set beliefs. These set beliefs create your reality. Your mind replays this reality to you. If you are a woman reading this you have a definition of what masculine is to you. You give this to men. During the First World War men who were pacifists and resisted war, and conscription, were given "white feathers" by women saying, "you are a coward, you will not defend your country." Women determine men's view of their masculine and feed this to men as men do to women.

Your society pitches women and men against each other to keep them polarized. This gives power to those who run your world. Definitions and stereotypes are hard to break when you feel you "expect" masculine behavior from "the masculine"; the man of the house. Ask is it coming from a cultural stereotype or does it foster the true "masculine" spirit in men and women who want integrated masculine energies.

The beginning of the true masculine identity begins in the heart for it is in your heart that your masculine identity is created. The heart knows why the soul has incarnated in the first place and the heart is the home of the integrated masculine spirit. You must feel free to allow the essence of the masculine heart to open. Your masculine heart is opening to the concept of a masculine identity, allowing the masculine identity to create with you brings you into a space of truth for the true masculine creative process.

Your masculine identity must begin by living in the heart with a space of truth being created for its mergence. Allow this concept to become "one" with you as you merge into oneness with all of life. Your life is now opening up to the masculine heart.

The masculine heart strengthens the feminine and allows it to receive. For example a mother can rest and nurture if her mate is at the ready protecting her feminine heart to grow it. This is time now to allow the masculine heart to open to the concept of growth and allowing the totality of human experience to merge into oneness with all of life.

As this transmission was being birthed, a student Lisa returned for more exploratory integration work with The High Priest. Her High Priest channeling's reveal: *"Lisa now has accessed the frequency of The High Priest and has applied to her life and world. Her world has changed because of The High Priest and she can look forward to creating more power, truth and increased life force with the High Priests energy."*

Lisa has been disciplined with her High Priests rituals giving them daily attention with her mystery school guides.

The High Priests were guiding me in teaching Lisa, and they said "The High Priest frequency will develop in you the ability to be able to discriminate with and offer power for your life of ascension. While creating with The High Priest you will be feeling energy blocks being released in the base chakra, the energy belt associated with self-nurturing."

Much of the training associated with The High Priest will involve the physical. Your body will be shifting in its alignment and you will feel more power and life force coming up through the legs and pelvic girdle, especially your hip bones and joints.

Your ability to be able to hold the High Priests frequency will be determined by your own unique relationship with your High Priest who will guide you through this process of self-discovery. In fact allowing the feeling of the masculine frequency to be around you will develop willpower and life force throughout your body, strengthening your resistance to the fears around the masculine principal generally.

The masculine principle is now under threat because it has been debased by men generally. Men are destroying the very thing that they have come in to learn. This is to learn how to like being a man and create through the masculine principle. Allowing a sense of inner stability in the masculine creates in men and women a sense of inner order and tranquility. Believing in your ability to develop the masculine allows now for the spirit of truth and trust to merge in oneness with all of life. The merging with all of life through the masculine principle brings to you a sense of completeness in the process of receiving.

You must try and find a space for receiving through the masculine process by allowing all love to infuse your cellular memory by infusing your cellular memory with the love of your land (home or adopted). Your belief in order through the balanced masculine will allow a shift in consciousness which brings protection to you and your loved ones.

Your protective qualities will be enhanced and you will want to find a space in your world for these qualities to develop. Protection implies respect for all life and all life is a protective and loving frequency. The essence of protection lies now in your ability to honor the masculine principal and live through this truth.

Your journey now is to really embrace the principle of true duality through the heart center. Your opportunity to draw on the energies for your heart activation and awakening cannot be over emphasized. You now need to feel the connectedness with all of life in the expression of purity in the masculine heart. The masculine heart is now able to be awakened in you by your attention to detail in the service of truth.

When you make a decision to "serve" truth you begin to awaken a dormant part of yourself. You begin to awaken to the mystery. The mystery is the spark of creation you need for your ascension and mergence into light. The soul becomes an expression of its androgynous self and you begin to feel that "you" can create this new self hood.

You are open to the creation process now in the spirit of the masculine and you need to feel the pleasure and excitement of allowing this principle of universal heart activation to take place. The spirit of the masculine lives in the universal heart.

Your essence through the universal heart only knows one thing and this is truth. The universal heart brings the essence of truth to you now as you awaken to the mystery. The expression of the masculine can be evoked through the spirit of trust and knowing that the purity of your heart will awaken the "true" masculine.

By observing all around you now, you are deepening your commitment to and awareness of The High Priest in you. You have had to undergo purification in many areas of your life to reach this point in your journey with The High Priest. The High Priest is now available for your mergence and ascension with him in this divine pure form. Your journey with him is now reaching a point where the collective consciousness of him in you becomes magnified. The essence of truth through this vibration is always there to create with you in love for the mystery for this is why you have found him.

His vibration is now surrounding you in love for the mystery and his truth creates the mystery in you. Your allowance for this to happen is to embrace the energy of truth for the mystery. The essence of the mystery is to live through the process of allowance. When you as "you" bring to your life "All Love" you open up to the essence of all loves in the receiving process and you must forge an identity with your High Priest now. There is a mergence with him taking place in you right now. The mergence brings truth into alignment with your soul's journey. This truth can be made manifest when you allow the message and the messenger to become one.

The message and messenger are allowing the truth to be revealed to you now. You are now finding focus and direction in the inner and outer manifestations of yourself now. You are one in essence with the High Priest. You are Love.

As your mergence with your High Priest consciousness is now taking place you will begin to remember who you truly are and you will allow the essence of who you are to bring to your life your truth. The vibration of truth is now one of power and light for whom you are and you must feel the essence of all love emerging in you now for your relationship with The High Priest to grow in you.

You need now to flow with this mergence for this is what it is, a mergence. You are now allowing the remembrance to take place and you will feel this remembrance in love for the mystery. The mystery of remembrance lies in truth made manifest and you are manifesting pure truth and love for your journey right now. The peace, space and love you give yourself now will enhance this mergence and the essence of all life will flower in you. You need now to really allow the activation process to take place within you now as you begin to spiral into the divine form the balanced masculine represents in you. You are now bringing down the vibration of truth and trust for mergence in you to be opening up the collective energy of The High Priest. The essence of this mergence lives in you now and your love for The High Priest.

The High Priest brings down this mergence now. You must allow yourself now to fully prepare yourself for this mergence and you must allow yourself to really bring through the spirit of peace and forgiveness for every aspect of the dark masculine which has hurt you. For you cannot ascend into mergence with The High Priest until this severance and mergence takes place. You must now ask for permanent severance from all dark masculine forces which have deliberately or unconsciously worked through others to destroy the energy the balanced masculine represents.

You must now feel the energy of all love around you and you must allow this energy to bring you all you need for your love. The essence of love is to live through the frequency of pure love for the mystery and the mystery is in you now for this mergence to take place. Allow the essence of all love to surround you, as this forgiveness takes place. You must now forgive all aspects of the dark masculine which has tried to destroy your truth. When this takes place mergence can take place. You are love.

By bringing to your heart now, your identity with your "masculine" self, your ability to heal your own karmic wounds is now taking place. You are now able to access a part of yourself that knows this and you are able also to believe in the spirit of true forgiveness. The essence of true forgiveness now brings to you a sense of true peace for the process of loving in your life. You are now in the process of this happening now.

The High Priest transmissions are a record of a journey for you now to embrace a part of yourself that needs healing. Your truth now is being explored by you and for the first time a record of your own inner journey can be accessed by yourself and revealed to yourself. Your truth now brings the light of spirit and true mergence with a part of yourself that only knows one thing. Love.

The gift of yourself to yourself now is to lovingly embrace The High Priest in all his aspects and forms. The essence of The High Priest lives through the spirit of true forgiveness for the masculine which as a term is misused and cannot be applied in your everyday application of words.

Allowing yourself now to explore this long-forgotten aspect of yourself is part of the remembrance process. For we are all here to remember. We have returned to remember and by being placed in a human body it is our opportunity to remember our power to live among the immortals.

Beginning your journey to explore yourself through the frequency of The High Priest is a belief in the power of your inner masculine and an acknowledgment that this power has a vibration that will heal and renew. To heal and renew brings you into resonance with all of life.

Your High Priest brings the essential balance back to you now for faith in who you are and a belief that what "you" are capable of. You must allow this belief to percolate your consciousness by meditating on the aspects of the High Priest's energy and making an intent for the masculine vibration to be part of your consciousness now. You are love.

While you are opening up to your new identity in the masculine frequency, you must observe where your old patterns create division and diversion. You are introducing yourself to a lost or forgotten part of yourself that only knows one thing and this is love. For your "mind" this is confusing and alien, for the language you are presenting it with only confuses it and it will rebel. You must allow for this and you must feel that you are truly free from this rebellious state or way of being. You need to really take yourself into a space of simple trust for this new view of yourself to take place and you must free yourself from your old patterns. For this to happen you must allow yourself peace and light to create your new reality through the heart for it is the heart, which knows this truth, and the heart, which hears the truth first.

Your first priority must be to ask yourself why you want the benefits of the masculine energy in the first place, and know it will help you.

Do this now, list your reasons?

Bringing through the might and power of the Priesthood and the sacred energy this balanced masculine represents will ensure immortality. Your belief in immortality is subjective; your reality tests your immortality every day. You are really challenging yourself to embrace the philosophy of living totally for your masculine self regardless of your human gender, for when you are able to do this you are embracing the world of mundane everyday reality as it is presented to you and superimposing your new relationship with yourself over yourself.

To believe such a thing is possible is creating in you a sense of oneness with all of life and a belief in the totality of everything. Every living thing has a part to play in the creation of yourself. Embracing the mysteries of the masculine implies you are at one with the forces which the masculine represent and you are allowed to open your lens wider to see life through the lens of the masculine.

You must feel the masculine merging into oneness with you as you set forth to allow this essence and spirit of yourself to bring you into resonance with all of life. The masculine principle lay behind your own personal evolution and every day "you" are being presented with this view of yourself.

Shaping your reality through the masculine principle brings you into resonance with every living thing. Every living thing embraces you when your identity goes beyond what our culture, sub conscious conditioning and family patterns dictate to you. The mystery of the masculine is embracing you now as you reach out to touch a part of yourself which feels this essence. For the feeling part of yourself you must embrace your identity now.

CHAPTER 6

Activating your Immortality

The mystery of the masculine entitles you to live as an immortal and to embrace your view of immortality as a shared truth between yourself and the universal forces which shape your destiny.

Allow the possibility of bringing through this mergence with your selves now. This integration of your "selves" brings you to a new knowing. A knowing of all there is and all of life for all of life is in this knowing. The knowing part of yourself now takes you to a new definition of who you truly are and brings you to a space of power and shared truth for your own love of yourself. To be able to reach into the part of yourself which knows and trusts this is an admittance that "you" are worthy to receive and give back to yourself the lost missing bits of your broken fragments and codings which see you at loss with an essential part of yourself.

The forces that shape your destiny are through the masculine essence of creation and these forces merge with you now as you bring to your world your truth. The essence of truth lives through the mystery, and you are opening now to receive through the vibration of the creative masculine. Allowing this spirit to merge with you now brings down power to shape your new identity. The essence of your new identity brings to you a space of growth and power and this energy is being made available to you now. You must feel this creative act of awareness in everything and you must allow this creativity to be part of your cellular memory right now. Your enactment of the masculine brings strength and power. You will feel an igniting in your energy centers and you will feel that you are bringing down the creative fire that fuels all life. All of life is fueled by the creative fire the masculine represents. You are allowing this essence to merge with you now. You are feeling this power, drive and energy and life force strengthen you and allow you the presence of all love to infuse your cellular memory now.

The fight for who you are becomes enacted through the masculine, the fight for your identity which shapes the forces of your humanness are beginning to awaken in you now.

Bringing this belief to you now reinforces in you power and peace and delight in the knowing that "you" are able to feel the essence of every living thing in you now. The forces shaping you now are reinforcing a belief in your identity. This identity is allowing you the belief that you are truly worthy to live your life wholly. Living your life wholly is the expression of your actuality. Your actuality is the sum total for who you ever were and who you aspire to. Your view of yourself is now allowing the essence of all light to create with you. You need now to allow the spirit of the masculine to really bring to your world the necessary ingredients to just love the person you are now. Loving this person is an act of love for yourself. The act of love for yourself brings to you now all you need to create a world of peace and order in your world.

The masculine principle is being presented to you now through the teachings of the ancient Priesthood to reinforce in you a belief that you are able to lovingly feel that the mystery of who you are is being presented to you. You are a belief in the sum total of yourself. Your "self" becomes alive when you acknowledge the masculine forces which shape your beingness.

This beingness has its birth in the essence of who "you" are and what "you" are capable of. Believing in this essence is your gift to yourself.

Allowing these sacred forces to shape your life leaves you open to receiving the power and gifts the balanced masculine creates in your worldview. You are now expanding your awareness of your totality and your expansion will bring new people and situations to your life to further expand and refine your view of your reality. You are opening up to this new view of yourself by being in the presence of "All Love" as a guide. "All Love" brings the truth behind the masculine to you as you are now feeling just what this energy can do to make you feel a sense of true masculine power. You are feeling the force of energy just envelope you now and in doing this you are showering yourself with light, peace and truth.

The energies that are being activated in you now are a powerful reminder of just who "you" are and why "you" need now to find the vibration of the masculine in your world view.

The masculine vibration is opening up your heart now, as you do not have a lopsided view of your world. For within you there is balance and truth emerging in your heart. This is a powerful time for this remembrance and in this "remembrance" you are feeling the energy of all life flow through you. Your DNA is being re-coded for this remembrance now. You are love.

The masculine principle is the force of creation and as it is a creative force it must be honored and respected every day. The honoring of the creative masculine spirit is the most powerful act you can do to bring down the forces through this principle which has at its source the principle of "All Love." "All Love" is a mighty force in the universe and you need now to just begin to allow this strength to find its way into your heart. The sun is the source of the creative masculine and must be evoked to allow the masculine spirit to unfold within you. Evoking the principle of life behind the sun and the great central sun is a ritual which can be undertaken at dawn. Sun salutations and sun worship are a common practice in many communities and in the ancient world practiced to the gods of the sun.

In Ancient Egypt, the Sun God Ra and Atum bring this life-affirming creative principle into focus.

Draw down the sun's power now. This increases the masculine life force as the moon's powers do the feminine life force. The power of the intelligent sun is streaming into your heart center now as it begins to pierce into your dark stagnant energies. Breath its rays into your heart now to really allow your skin to tingle and become "alive" to its vigor, force and light. Its unbelievable light and power light up every cell and atom in your body, bringing masculine renewal and strength.

You are now opening up to the magical universe where the mystery of creation can be revealed to you. The High Priest's masculine force and presence is around you now as you consciously and deliberately challenge yourself to step into this new view of yourself. Just being in the presence of these amazing and powerful magical practices brings you into a new relationship with yourself and your world. Your relationship with this new view of yourself and your world now opens up a new aspect of your life and reality and you are now in the company of some mighty and powerful magicians. These magicians will reveal aspects of themselves to you in various forms for different intents. You are bringing down to your world the essence of what human potential is capable of because you are in the presence of these magical forces which shape your destiny and that of your world.

The Magician Priest was an awesome presence to behold and you are engaging with these presences when you align to your magical practices of the ancient world. This power is settling on your aura because "you" are bringing to your world the realization of your human potential. This potential is a mighty responsibility, as you become a sacred vessel for truth.

Through this truth, you are bringing to your world your relationship with your magical potential through the masculine forces. The vibration can be worked to help you realize your own power, truth and light and to bring light and strength to the world you live in.

Allowing the space to surrender to your own humanness is a pre-requisite for The High Priest's frequency to merge with you. The feeling of just being in a protective mantle The High Priest embraces, gives you a sense of security in your world. This is a time now to feel this sense of peace and wonder for the Priest's sacred presence in your life. Your oneness with The High Priest will extend into everything you do, say and feel. Your love, peace and respect for yourself as an integrated human being grows and you are opening up to mighty forces which support your essence. This essence has its outlet in everything and is everything. The essence of everything is contained in this delicate balance of universal energies pouring into you now. Your essence merges in oneness with the essence of all love and you are observing your humanness through the eyes of your own real self. The vibration reinforces and stabilizes your energy field, life force and your intent can be manifested.

You can have intent, but if it isn't manifested by being grounded into the Earth it stays where it is. The frequency of the balanced masculine balances this intent by earthing it. The greatest achievements on Earth are intent manifested. The essence of intent is to allow the power of the intent to be manifested through The High Priest's frequency.

The masculine principle is intent manifested. I manifest my intent through the masculine principle.

Manifesting intent for the higher good of yourself brings you into a space of truth for the mystery. The mystery is within you and the mystery becomes you through manifested intent. Allowing this frequency to really become one with your essence will bring you power to achieve all your aims in life.

The secret of manifesting lies in intent. Your intent must be grounded through the masculine principle. Allowing this view of your humanness to encompass this life force will allow you to step into the vibration of real power and light for your journey now. This vibration is being made available to you now while you bring the forces of "All Love" into play.

All of life is intent manifested. Try it. Imagine you need something (i.e. a new job, car, relationship, etc._

Your intent has been spoken.

"I intend that I manifest this intent through the opening of my creative masculine."

"My creative masculine is now opening me to intend that my manifestation will be part of the intent process."

"I lovingly allow myself this change in circumstances to bring me closer to my truth."

"I love myself enough to deserve this, and I do deserve to experience everything possible in my world, which brings me closer to my truth."

The forces that shape your destiny lie inside you and every moment is precious alchemy to help you reveal yourself to yourself. Your ability to really feel where "you" are at, at any given moment, allows the spirit of all life to unfold within you.

For example, you are being challenged at any moment, not by the other person, but by yourself to reveal yourself to yourself. At any moment you can have this aspect of yourself revealed to you and you are then able to witness the alchemy of yourself in this moment.

The creative masculine spirit through The High Priest is able to cut through this illusion and bring you back again to a state of knowing yourself enough to be able to "see" through this illusion. You must feel the essence of yourself embrace this "untidy" part of your thought pattern, this meandering thought which got out of the cage. See this thought as being like a sheep, which has escaped from the flock. Your creative masculine is the guard dog that is sent on a mission to bring the stray animal back to the group. (The stray animal being your untidy parts.)

At any moment you/your emotion can bolt, something will trigger it; an unresolved aspect of yourself is about to create havoc, spoiling the order you have an identification with, for example (the guard dog). You must be alert at every moment, for if too many sheep follow the one who has escaped, then the group aim has broken down.

Throughout your life you are constantly being reminded of this and every second is precious alchemy to bring order, peace and stillness. Managing one thought is enough; just keep your observation of your emotions constantly connected to your High Priest.

In a magnificent shrine on Mt. Kurama, Japan there is an Amida Buddha of compassion gazing down lovingly upon those who kneel in front of him. He is still and loving, a peaceful presence, reminding you to always remember you are under his watchful guardianship.

Extended from his hand is a golden rope and you as a worshiper are invited to hold the rope and feel the connection between his hand, which holds the rope, and your hand. Feel this now. The still loving presence of "All Love," represented by the statue, the benevolence of his shining eyes toward you. You hold the rope, and it connects to his hand and to his heart. This energy is available through the loving presence now as you hold yourself "together" while the thought can be reigned in or brought home again. This energy will bring you back to yourself when you are struggling with too many complicated thoughts swimming in your head.

The joy of remembering this presence keeps you in a space of completeness for all there is. You need to really feel now the vibration of this essence represented by The High Priest's sacred presence, bring you to a space within yourself which knows this and responds to the call of this balance and essence within yourself. Your love is reminding you of the purity and trust of all love your newly developing masculine is showing you right now.

Your love for yourself must always be acknowledged when you are doing initiatory exploratory journeying such as this, for it is pioneering and challenges all previously held definitions of who "you" are.

You are opening up now to the vibration of "All Love" and "All Love" through the presence of the sacred divine masculine is expressing itself in every way in your life right now. This expression has its outlet through the vibration of stillness and peace for who you are right now. Bringing you to your world right now is the knowledge that your High Priest's energy is going to bring to you the absolute essence of who you are, because regardless of your human gender you need to be introduced to this power at some point in your newly emerging self. Your conscious now is opening you up to the essence of all love and you are feeling the power of all love around you now.

The frequency of the balanced masculine allows the forces of nature to be balanced in your world. Imagine a group of people with their masculine energies balanced holding energy with concentration and intent for balance in their natural world. This should be a priority in your consciousness as balancing and clearing your environment from pollutants, discordant weather patterns and energetic disturbances through people's thoughts is essential to your planet's evolution.

If you want to do this as a group, gather on an auspicious time (i.e. full moon, dark moon and new moon, etc.). These natural monthly occurrences bring you into resonance with the Earth's atmosphere and is a powerful reminder to keep you connected to your Earth.

Early morning dawn sun rituals create life force and power brings you into a space of purity and truth for the sacredness of your Earth and its people. Humans are all responsible for our Earth's balance, not the demonic leaders who try to manipulate the energy of others for control and domination. This is time for your inner masculine strength to bring you into resonance with your Earth and the responsibility you have in maintaining this energy balance.

CHAPTER 7

The Divine Masculine

The Divine Masculine as a philosophy and way of being is being encoded upon you now as you merge in oneness with all of life. The essence of all life lies in the mystery and the spirit of all love lies in this truth. You are feeling the need to really own the part of yourself which knows this truth and respects it. Bringing yourself to a space of acceptance for who "you" are is now allowing "yourself" to grow.

Believing in this acceptance and love just allows the essence of yourself to merge into oneness with all there is. You are now radiating the life force, energy and power in all of life and all of life brings you to a state of oneness for every living thing. The essence of every living thing lies in the mystery and you are vibrating to this consciousness now. Being in a space of wonder and stillness allows the spirit and beauty of who "you" are to bring your own magical essence and uniqueness to all of life. All of life radiates to your love of self and you are one in essence with all of life. Allowing the spirit and oneness to surround you now allows the spirit of the divine masculine to begin to radiate from you.

Your power, longevity and life force will increase as you are integrating your spirit into matter and the oneness with everything becomes evident. Your love and strength brings peace, purity and power in the masculine process.

Beginning to allow the vibration of your sacred essence to envelope you now allows for surrender to take place and bring you to a space of forgiveness for yourself. Allowing yourself now to forgive yourself for every little thing keeps you in a space of purity and light for the mystical journey you are embarking on to reclaim this lost part of yourself. You are feeling now the essence and wonder in all of life create with you now for mystery of who you are and you are beginning to find this sacred essence everywhere and in everything. The purity of your intent to bring in the balanced masculine allows your energy and life force to multiply bringing you vigor, strength, vitality and powerful life-affirming energy.

This vibration is accelerating your path and you are vibrating to the essence of all life in the sacred mystery of who you are. This essence energy and life force is being made available to you now as you open to the mystery of the balanced masculine The High Priest represents.

This is a might, force and power that bring you into a complete state of resonance for who you are and what you are capable of. You are one with this magical universe now as you begin to allow yourself the essence of all love to surround you now.

The beauty of your new mergence with the frequency of the masculine will bring magnetic energy to you and you will be able to channel more light. More power and life force will fill your energy field. You will be very quickly manifesting the energy of the universal heart frequency to you, as you will be opening your heart and the hearts of others. You are opening up your heart to receive the energy of all love and you will be now experiencing a powerful current of power, energy and light. All around you will vibrate energy, power and life force and you will feel the essence of this life force around you.

Begin to breathe in this power through visualizing the sun, the source of power and light in your aura now. Feel the essence of the sun, its fiery core, and its nucleus vibrating to your heart's essence and allow the essence of its energy to lock into your heart. Your heart's energy connects to the source of all light, the source of the sun, and you must feel this energy pulling you to a space of oneness for all the billions of suns in our galaxy and beyond. Our vibration is matching the universal vibration of the suns from our Milky Way. Visualize 100 billion stars, suns vibrating to your energy field and hold the consciousness for this expansion of your awareness right now. Our bodies are stardust and contain the same elements as the suns. These living presences are available for you now to connect with and magnify your energy field, bringing in the power, joy and completeness of the balanced masculine. Take the sun into the fiery core of the Earth and blend the two. Just visualize the sun streaming through you, then sending it into the heart of the Mother Earth. Hold the frequency through your intent and concentration. Feel this now. Down into the fiery heart of the Earth, your mother, you bring the powerful masculine forces of the sun, your father. Feel them merge and unite. You are part of the mystery of creation and all there is. This is a most strengthening time for you as you open your heart to the sun's heart. The heart of the sun is in our heart as you allow the essence of its mergence to be "one" with "you."

Your relationship with yourself is always under examination. In opening up to new energies the balanced masculine represents, you will be undergoing a process of purification. The essence of your relationship needs purification when you are shifting gears and opening up to new energies. It is important that you bring this new relationship with yourself into resonance with all of life and that all of life supports and respects your journey. The essence of the love supports your journey when you are undergoing purification. The purification of yourself to a process which must be undertaken when you are opening up to the new energies is what The High Priest represents.

Rituals of purification were performed before all initiations and the ancient world had many such rituals. Right now as you open your heart to yourself you are undergoing purification. The essence of purification is essential for you to hold and carry this new frequency. This ritual of purification will be given to you now to help you open up and draw down the powers of the divine masculine.

Water bathing with your intent to purify yourself is an important admission to the light beings that you are sincere. Bathing is a purification ritual when it sets out to bring the sun's purpose into resonance with your truth. Bathing in the sea is an important spiritual undertaking; this can be done at dawn or in the moonlight by the full moon. Dawn bathing in the sacred river The Ganges is a daily ritual for many Hindus. The bathing Ghats at Varanasi, India, the city of the dead, create an atmosphere of purification for the initiate. All rituals involving bathing are considered sacred in ancient cultures.

The High Priests have a sacred lake in Karnak temple complex in Luxor, Egypt. (Previously known as Thebes in Ancient Egypt) where Priests undertook ritual baths. All rituals involving purification involve water.

To be in the presence of the ancient ones is a privilege, and you must feel that you can develop a relationship similar to a friendship with the particular group of beings assigned to you. The soul group will be activated by your intent and you may like to feel the essence of yourself merge with them. The feeling aspect of yourself must be evoked. You must feel you want to be in the company, energy of these wondrous beings who can bring to your life your truth. The truth of your human life must now be in unison with the energies of The High Priest and the sacred ones; this relationship is a gradual one and emerges fully over time. You are encoding on your cellular memory this truth and your energy is opening up to what can be achieved when you create with these vibrations.

Allowing yourself the essence of who you are create with you, brings peace, power and purity to you and you are able to feel lighter and more peace filled every time you evoke these wondrous beings for they have the same purpose of creating with you to evolve yourself and your world.

Embodying The Divine Masculine of All Truth, Through The High Priest

By bringing their vibration into your life you are allowing the sense of a magical new reality to be part of your whole being. Your world becomes one with all the forces assisting you in mergence with the essence of all love.

Your new view opens up your potential to create at an unbelievable rate, your ascension process accelerates and you just become united with the power of powers with the sacred divine masculine.

The spirit of awareness is all around you when you bring to your world the power available to you. The power available to you brings you home to yourself and your own mergence into your own true masculine power is just so powerful for your ascension. You are striving now for this energy to bring you to a state of completion for who you really are and what you are capable of. Your energy power and drive brings you into resonance with all life and all of life protects and supports your identity in the masculine right now.

The ancient priesthood is creating with you all the time you acknowledge this undiscovered part of yourself and you must stand guard and be ready for the new energies pouring into you right now.

Your energy is drawing you even further to an undiscovered part of yourself that knows this anyway. You are now bringing to your world this power, and it will attract to you other powerful magnetic beings to you. Your ability to manifest for your own new life even brings you closer to who you really are and your knowing that you are capable of absolutely everything you need for your truth is magical to behold. You become one in the essence with the sacred ones.

Bringing now to your world is the opportunity to assist in all of creation. You are now part of the creative force magnifying itself through the High Priest's energy. Allow this power to surge through you now. Bring this power to you to allow you to be the warrior in your life and your world.

You need to really feel the force of the energies to create with you and bring you into a space of purity and love for all there is. Bringing down these energies allows for all love to surround you and you need to know this energy will drive you into parts of yourself that already know this truth. The essence, energy and life force of your life now, become your friends and guides. The essence of yourself becomes revealed to you and you are now participating in a worldview which needs your vigor, power and drive. Believing in your new magical essence is opening you up even further into your new magical life. Your power now is beginning to be felt and you will feel the enormity of what can be achieved in your life.

You are now just concentrating on your own power through the High Priest's energy. Believing in this power that you are of the sacred essence of the priesthood will attract people to who will feel it as well through you. Your view of this vibration is there regardless of your gender.

Believing in such a reality is the beginning of change and your belief in this vibration brings you even closer to all you could possibly wish for. For belief and faith keeps your heart pure, not corrupted and you will be able to realize the essence of yourself. The true essence of yourself is revealed to you in this moment. The moment is upon you now to seize the opportunity these extraordinary energies give you.

When you were a child your view of reality was determined by your environment (i.e. where you lived, your immediate surroundings and your family). Now as an adult you are in a position to challenge your child-like view of your reality which isn't this world at all. Your view of "your world" is not this world, the Earth world, but every living thing. Every living thing participates with you in this view of the world right now as you open up even further to the mysteries. The essence of the mysteries lies in the view of the world that brings you peace, hope and renewal for your life.

Allowing this to take place brings you closer to "your" true reality, the reality of a world that is not contained by someone else's definition of your world. Your worldview is yours and you are allowed to shape this reality. You are allowed to create with it and you are able to make "it" your "world."

Your consciousness is expanding and limitless.

The presence of the ancient Priesthood through the Divine Masculine will begin to become encoded in your cellular memory now and you will begin to feel the life-changing results.

Firstly you are now a magician and as a magician you can change consciousness for your higher good and truth as well as the higher good and truth for others on the path of being human.

A magician heals. Your magical healing abilities will strengthen and you will be able to heal your own body, mind and spirit. A new sense of peace and order will become "one" with you and you will begin to allow your world to develop relationships with the cosmic forces which shape our universe.

Your ability to shape-shift, create new realities and bring love to your world. Love then becomes an everyday occurrence. Your life begins to gather momentum. Life moves very quickly and you will become known for power to create peace, order and harmony in your world. Your heart is opening every time you work with your rituals to your High Priest and your intent magnifies and grows. Grow your power to love the creation that is you and bring to your world all you have learned in your journey. Your love of all life is around you and you will allow the precious gift of whom you are to bring you to a space where the mystery and you are one.

Shape shifting is changing your reality and allowing the essence of the Divine Masculine to enter you and bring down energy for your manifestation. All of life is a manifestable process. From the moment we are born we are manifesting. By manifesting through the masculine you are shifting into a new reality, a new way of being human.

To be an open channel for The High Priest's energy you need to develop a strong relationship with your heart as the heart is the way to your power and truth.

A person cannot shape shift for manifestation unless the heart is fully engaged in the process. The process of engaging our heart brings you to a space of awareness in every area of your life. Your life is one truth in the manifesting process. The manifesting ability for you as a channel for the Divine Masculine is one of truth and power. The essence of your truth through The High Priest's energy is realized when you have full authority over all aspects of your inner masculine. Bringing this energy, power and life force to you now reinforces the true essence of the masculine.

To be able to feel all aspects of your masculine gives you power in your world and you can create a reality which brings you closer to your truth.

Your life must reflect truth. You want to find within yourself peace and you must now allow this peace to unfold around you. For you to live with this sense of peace and order is to respect the essence of all life and keep the sacred essence of all life deep within your heart, bringing now to your life empowerment. Empowerment implies respect for all living things to live their lives on this Earth. Your power to feel a sense of detachment, peace and order will reflect how you have lived with the Divine Masculine. The Divine Masculine just keeps growing in you when you respect the essence of all life to bring you home to your truth. The vibration of pure trust must unfold around you now as you allow the truth of the Divine Masculine to bring you to a complete circle within yourself for you are now within this complete circle now as you journey deep into your heart. Your heart's chambers share in their memory knowledge of your power and abuse. Self abuse of this power, from your "self" to yourself is felt by the heart. It is time now to really allow this essence and truth to bring you home to yourself. You are one in essence with truth now, as you awaken up your cellular memory to reclaim this lost part of yourself.

Allowing the spirit of light to create with you brings you now allowance to begin your mission to truth. The aim of truth is to live with the sacred Divine Masculine and encode it into your totality, for there can be no other way. To live with this truth now implies that you must release and surrender your previously held definition of what it is to be even human. Your allowance of bringing these new frequencies to you makes your gift to yourself a complete one and you are beginning now to allow the secret sacred self to emerge.

You are now feeling the need to really tap into this rich vein of raw masculine power which brings you to a space of love and forgiveness of yourself. Your journey now must encompass this truth. Your journey must allow for this truth to emerge. Beginning to open up to your truth brings you peace, profound peace and light. Light, peace and power are yours when you embrace this sacred part of yourself. This sacred part of yourself now knows no bounds as you open up even further to "your mystery," your own sacred secret mystery. Allowing makes all things possible. By allowing the secret part of yourself is made manifest and you can really begin your mergence and journey into light.

To begin now to allow the experience of unity in your self will bring the magical essence of the ancient Priests to you for all you need for your life. The essence of the Priesthood lives in your essence and your willingness to allow this way of being will envelope you in all love for all there is. The frequency you have allowed yourself to be attuned to brings you to a space of purity for all there is.

Allowing this purity to be part of your cellular memory recodes to all there is and you will bring to your world the essence of who "you" truly are. Allowing this essence to envelope you brings you to a state of knowing for all there is and your must feel that the energy and life force brings you to a space of knowing that "you" can have all you need for your magical world. For your life now embraces this way of being and you must allow this sacred essence of all life through the masculine frequency to envelop you and create all you need for your love-filled journey.

You are releasing your identification with anything that is not of the light and you must allow the essence of "All Love" to surround you. The magical Priesthood is waiting for your soul to awaken from its slumber and inertia so you can join with this undiscovered part of yourself. You are free to envelope yourself in this energy now for you are opening your heart to yourself.

Thank the Divine Masculine guides for their gift to you by acknowledging to yourself that you truly allow the sacred essence of the ancient Priesthood to be with you right now. Begin now to just get started to take your journey outward in the new way of experiencing your humanness. Every opportunity now should be to awaken this powerful and mysterious force within you. Awakening this sacred energy is an act of reverential love for you from you and you are opening up to this extraordinary portal of raw masculine power being made available to you right now.

What is it you must give yourself in this act of love and forgiveness of yourself to receive the love of the ancient ones the Priesthood represents?

Begin now to allow this new view of your world to create with you.

This visualization exercise will support your connection with the Divine Masculine:

Go out into nature to a place undisturbed by others at dawn.

Get the exact time of the sunrise.

Begin a small ritual at sunrise as it begins its journey over the horizon.

Your ritual is an offering to the masculine forces of the sun to assist you now. Your offering of yourself as a channel or vessel for the sacred Divine Masculine will begin now to awaken you to the potential of your life when the masculine is evoked. By allowing this to happen you are surrendering to the power and light the ancients will bring you.

Right now you are vibrating to the frequency of The High Priest and you will now find the essence of all life flow through you. You are opening yourself to the essence of yourself and you are now feeling a sense of completion for all there is. You are now asking yourself why you are allowing so many aspects of your old world to be part of the new reality you have begun to explore. Your new reality is a gift to yourself to begin the journey of self development to multi- dimensionality as a way of being. You are opening up the doorway to a magical universe; one of power, strength and light and you are demanding more from yourself.

Right now, you are experiencing a sense of power and goundedness you never thought possible and you are beginning to experience life in a way you never believed. Believing in this power and what it will bring you leads you to a space of pure delight for being human. It is a magical time to feel so earthed in your reality and be able to accept this earthed new you. The energy of the Earth becomes one with you and you are feeling now your belief in yourself will bring you to a space of purity and trust for all there is. Your magical essence becomes "alive" and you are "alive" to every possibility life presents you with. Your magical powers with reality and truth begin to manifest and the world of multi-dimensionality will really emerge as you journey into the heart of yourself.

Allowing yourself now to create with your High Priest will bring you this magical power and you will begin to really grow up to a universal way of being human. This universality has its core a knowing that you are bringing to your world power and truth. For without power and truth you cannot manifest or be the person you want to be in your totality. Just accepting now that you are bringing to your world this power allows the precious gift of alchemy to create with you and you must be aware or now you are going to challenge your previously held belief about your ability to really get to the core of belief patterns which have had their roots in old fears established a long time ago. You must always monitor these fears and seek to go beyond them. You need now to really establish this core link with yourself as you monitor your old belief patterns and limiting structures about your ability to receive. For when you allow yourself to receive you are in the company of some mighty energies which will bring to you all you need for your journey to the heart of yourself. The heart of yourself knows one truth, and this is the truth of the self. The self must be truthful to itself or the core of you cannot be strong enough to allow the frequency of The High Priest to enter.

Right now the energy transmission from The High Priest is shape shifting your reality, and you are seeing your world in a completely new way. You need now to really feel this and open up to the experience this shape shifting of yourself entails, and you must allow the precious gift of alchemy to create with you. This powerful new reality is what The High Priest brings. Your allowance of this new reality to take place will reinforce in your life peace and order, but above all power, for it is power which is the core of the High Priest's relationship with "you."

All of life is a power struggle at some level and all of life creates with you at the level of truth you are able to carry. This is an important time to really bring this power to you and you must seek to really bring the essence of it into your world. Just receiving the precious gift of power through The High Priest you are realizing an important aspect of your reality with The High Priest's power at your disposal to create with. Believing in your own power to generate energy with The High Priest will bring additional life force and energy to your entire being and it is in this cellular matrix that you can begin to merge in oneness for all there is. Allowing the essence of you to create with you is the truth made manifest. This truth has its beginnings in the essence self, the seed self and your reality is now encompassing this new way of being. The new state of mergence is upon you now as you witness your life unfolding to bring your full self, your totality in view. You are presenting yourself to yourself and you must feel the essence of all life truly unfold around you to develop this unique and special view you have of yourself now. This journey will be taking you into uncharted parts of yourself and you must feel now the essence of all life unfold around you to bring you into a state of awareness for all around you.

Embodying The Divine Masculine of All Truth, Through The High Priest

Believing in this new reality of the Divine Masculine through The High Priest is challenging core beliefs about your identity in a real and tangible way. This expression of yourself in this new form can be made manifest in your everyday totality.

The sum experience of all you ever have been will open up to you in a way which reflects your new magical world. This magical universe now is beginning to unfold within you and you are always going to feel the essence of truth around you. For the liberation now brings to you a true sense of truth and order of course unimaginable power. Thus living essence is yours now. You have awakened to the mystery of The High Priest and the Divine Masculine.

Part III:
The High Priest Lessons

Lesson One:

Emotions

When you want to create a relationship with your High Priest, there are certain emotions you may wish to reflect on and develop within yourself. Some of these emotional attributes are listed below. Please tick the appropriate boxes.

Do you allow yourself to experience emotions in a way which respects your truth?
☐ Never ☐ Sometimes ☐ Always

Are you fearful of your own emotions getting out of control?
☐ Never ☐ Sometimes ☐ Always

Do you feel you have to have "control" in all of life?
☐ Never ☐ Sometimes ☐ Always

Is "control" your weapon?
☐ Never ☐ Sometimes ☐ Always

Do you feel you have to be in "control" in relationships?
☐ Never ☐ Sometimes ☐ Always

Do you stay still and contemplate all around you, daily?
☐ Never ☐ Sometimes ☐ Always

Do you feel you have enough structure and order in your life?
☐ Never ☐ Sometimes ☐ Always

Do you see the world solely as "man's" creation?
☐ Never ☐ Sometimes ☐ Always

If you have answered "Sometimes" or "Always" you are now ready to explore the world of The High Priest.

The High Priest is a spiritual being who is able to help you bring balance, love and abundance into your life. In other words, he teaches you to like yourself and your humanness. To begin to develop your relationship with your High Priest you may like to consider offering him a small gift or offering, such as a crystal, feather, incense etc. You may have a pendant or amulet you wish to offer as your respect for the teachings of The High Priest. You become "his" student/friend. He becomes your mentor, coach and trainer. The offering is an acknowledgement of respect for your role and his teachings.

(1) Would you describe yourself as a "Truth-Seeker?" YES/NO

(2) Do you react "truthfully" to situations where you feel threatened or challenged? YES/NO

In matters of truth most of us to some degree tell "white lies." However, it is your emotional "reaction" which determines your ability to be able to create with your High Priest. When you consistently tell "white lies," you will have to really begin to challenge your definition of truth.

(3) Who do you tell "white lies" to? Your boss, wife, lover or child. The list can be as long as you like, this is handing over your power to that person.

(4) Circle the qualities you would most like to have if you felt more empowered, or felt you had inner truth with this person.

  A) Stability
  B) Power
  C) Balanced emotions
  D) Honesty
  E) Strength
  F) Open Hearted
  G) Other

Now prioritize these in order of importance (A-G). A being most needed G being least needed.

What you need to do is to allow these "truth-filled" experiences to happen to you energetically within yourself first. This is very important as it is creating The High Priest in you first. It is a little like a rehearsal. Try to imaginatively enter into the space where you need to find your High Priest's qualities. Breathe deeply, powerfully, rhythmically three times to establish this "inner space." Do this now.

Imagine the last encounter where you felt challenged. Visualize this scene with the person in front of you. Re-create the scene, detail for detail. Now feel yourself breathing deeply, powerfully and rhythmically, creating with your High Priest as an imaginary figure.

Do this now. Re-create the scene and feel The High Priest inside you. Go through the scene with "him" and feel yourself drawn to "his" power and all the gifts you have allowed yourself to receive from him.

(5) (a) I want you to describe, either through a fictional character (i.e. a movie star, myth, legend) or in someone you know who has these attributes listed above, while creating this new scene. If you don't know anyone or can't imagine anyone with these qualities, just create a fictional character and describe him now.

(5) (b) Now you have created your ideal character by doing this exercise, you can decide now how you want him to behave when you are challenged by your own emotions and give your authority away. The next time you are challenged by a man or woman, you need to remember how your ideal character would behave:

(6) When you feel challenged, you must remember to give yourself space to be you. In point form, list 5 steps that you can incorporate into a situation where you find yourself "controlling" or being "in the mind." How do you see yourself reacting? What steps are you taking to give yourself this space? (i.e. breath, visualization, make an appointment to discuss the issue at a certain time and date, etc.)

(7) Ask yourself now can the person who challenges you surrender his/her ego and let go to enter your space? More importantly, are you allowing yourself your own space first? By re-creating the scene, you will learn to trust yourself in the next situation you feel challenged. Record, in detail, your responses below to see where you were challenged.

A) I couldn't go through it
B) I felt too much fear in doing it
C) I achieved my aims and felt empowered
D) Other

If you want to further develop your relationship with your High Priest and bring balanced love into your life, you will now begin to make a commitment to creating with him by asking your Higher Self's permission to begin your relationship with him. Your High Priest will create with your Higher Self. Your Higher Self is your "soul," or unconscious self. Establish this first. You can do this by going into a meditation and just feeling or sensing the Higher Self. Your Higher Self is your first contact and will help you develop your soul's journey on Earth.

(8) Your "Higher Self" exercise needs to be completed now.

* Begin your breathing technique outlined earlier in this lesson and establish your connection with the Higher Self.

* Focus on the crown chakra.

* Draw an indigo or dark violet yin/yang symbol over your crown now.

* Feel the energy of doing this right now. Even though you can't see the results yet, the Higher Self will be activated and ready to give you the go-ahead for all you need in your journey with the High Priest.

* When you sense a tingle or a shift in energy, you will know you have communicated with your Higher Self.

The High Priest teaches you to control the forces within you by controlling others, and develops your essence, your creative function and power, with no fear of truth. The High Priest is a powerful man; a truth-seeker and will not compromise the "self." Men feel they must control in order to receive. List the people you feel you have to control in order to feel "a man." Is it fear of losing control and becoming "emotional," with the world not being solely "your" creation?

Your High Priest through your Higher Self teaches you one very important gift. This is the gift to bring truth to every situation. Love is the energy, which carries truth, and love is the most important ingredient for truth to be realized.

To make a commitment to The High Priest you can establish breathing rituals every day and use the Breath of Fire exercise to fire up your belly. The last exercise outlined in Chapter 1 will be an excellent start for this personal relationship with your High Priest to be developed.

You can further connect to the life-giving powers of The High Priest by performing Sun Salutations to your High Priest. If you are not familiar with these yoga poses, they can be easily taught by a yoga teacher. They are also known as Tibetan Rejuvenation Rites. Ten minutes per day is ideal, in the early morning light or at sunrise if possible.

Summary

You will complete this lesson by completing the following:

- your "white lies" list of authority figures
- your list of preferences for your own power
- your fictional character
- listing 5 steps to give yourself space
- your 100-word response to being challenged — self-review
- your 200-word response for those you need to control in order to feel a "man"
- your Breath of Fire ritual
- your 10-minute Sun Salutations daily

Congratulations!
You are now allowing yourself to realize your creative potential.

Lesson 2:

Shifting Your Reality

Your world will begin to change now that you have begun to establish your relationship with your High Priest. You will find that you are drawing new people into your life and that your old life is shifting. You are becoming more observational of people and your responses to them.

(1) Describe either in point form or in a couple of sentences how your old world has begun to change.

(2) You might like to discuss your observations of your "new" truthful self.

By observing and challenging your old patterns, you will begin to receive more from your High Priest. By feeding your High Priest with power and light, you will be enacting your creative masculine spirit, like a Fire God.

Can you demonstrate to yourself now how your practice of devotion to your High Priest can be achieved in the scarab visualization (i.e. by practicing it every day for 14 days sequentially?)

Try and imagine now being able to create this creative masculine visualization for your High Priest any time during your day, by imagining your spine radiating this energy throughout your day.

(3) Whenever you are feeling stressed, you can activate your scarab, to begin this journey to your heart squeezing his emerald fluid into your heart muscles. **Imagine your High Priest beside you giving you instructions from his visualization, calling him when you are stressed and want "control." Give yourself time to really acknowledge to yourself that you have clearly lost your control, or mind scenarios, and moved onto the heart with the emerald green fluid in the heart. List 5 examples:**

(4) The High Priest states that men have been fed a false reality. Can you demonstrate how you may have been fed a false reality of your manhood, by your father, teachers, media, etc.?

(5) What part of your life is not working for you right now? (i.e. relationships, financials, etc.)

(6) What parts could be made simpler if you were "truthful" to yourself?

The High Priest will give you these gifts.

1. Magnetic power. You become a magnetic energetic presence.

2. You will become a man to yourself; this man will be the real essence of your manhood.

3. Do you know the difference between men "controlling others" and magnetic energy?

Can you imagine yourself possessing magnetic energy instead of aggression and attitude, which is controlling?

4. Do you crave freedom? I mean true inner freedom?

5. If you could, would you change your career?

These are the gifts from your High Priest, if you wish to accept these gifts, you must acknowledge in some way to your High Priest you will use and appreciate the gifts he is giving you. By accepting these gifts you are acknowledging to yourself that you are able to change what others have taught you to be.

The only thing your High Priest wants from you is your ability to love yourself enough to say "yes" to his gifts. Gifts always bring responsibilities. In your relationship with your High Priest, the gift is the responsibility to really express pain, the pain of not allowing yourself to receive these gifts. We can be offered gifts, but the pain often stops us from expressing our gratitude for the gifts being offered. If you can honestly say "yes" to the gifts you will have to release attachments. In your life now being human brings attachments to everything. Your new gifts from your High Priest will challenge these attachments.

It is time now to examine your world for distractions, which prevent you from being "truthful." By tracking your whole life, you can begin to see the pattern of where masculine enslavement began. When you choose your career, this is the first choice in determining how you will perform in the world.

(7) When did you first become aware of the reality that is essentially corrupt? (i.e. politically, environmentally, spiritually) Was this in primary school, high school, university, other?

(8) While you don't have to do a physical fire walking exercise, The High Priest states that you will be born through the vibration of fire. Fire is the first element to be faced in ascension. **What fire exercises have you completed to remove the dross and purify?**

(9) Are you able to devote 10 minutes a day in your private devotional space to your High Priest? Where is this devotional space? What does it have in it? Describe in as much detail as possible the space.

(10) (a) What "illusions" do you hold about cars/women/sex?

What do they mean to you? Ask yourself; how do I control these distractions?

This of course does not mean you deny yourself these gifts, but how often would you ask; is this right? Does this feel right?

| |
| |

(10) (b) Who has cheated your heart? Why? Can you see where you gave your power away?

| |
| |

Summary

- Your scarab visualization
- Activate your heart through the "emerald" scarab
- Your 50 words on false reality/life not working and "truth" exercise
- Were your 5 gifts challenging? Did you accept them?
- Your 50 words on career choice and external reality questions.
- Your 50 words on fire walking exercise.
- Your 100 words on devotional space.
- Your 2 exercises on illusion and cheating your heart.

Lesson 3:

Enacting the Masculine Principle

As you are beginning to find strength and power with your High Priest, you can now focus on exactly what your training regime will entail. Your High Priest is your first trainer. He will be introducing you to specialists, who can further help you embody the principles of truth. Ptah the Ancient Egyptian God is such energy.

(1) How did you feel when you were "told" that your tree roots needed to be ripped out? Whose expectations of you are you carrying from "loved" family members?

(2) How do you feel with your family tree gone? (scared, released, powerful, liberated, didn't want to look at it, etc.)

(3) Where in your body do you feel most vulnerable? Look at bones, breaks, childhood injuries, skeletal structure, and weakness in joints. Draw yourself as a skeleton.

Embodying The Divine Masculine of All Truth, Through The High Priest

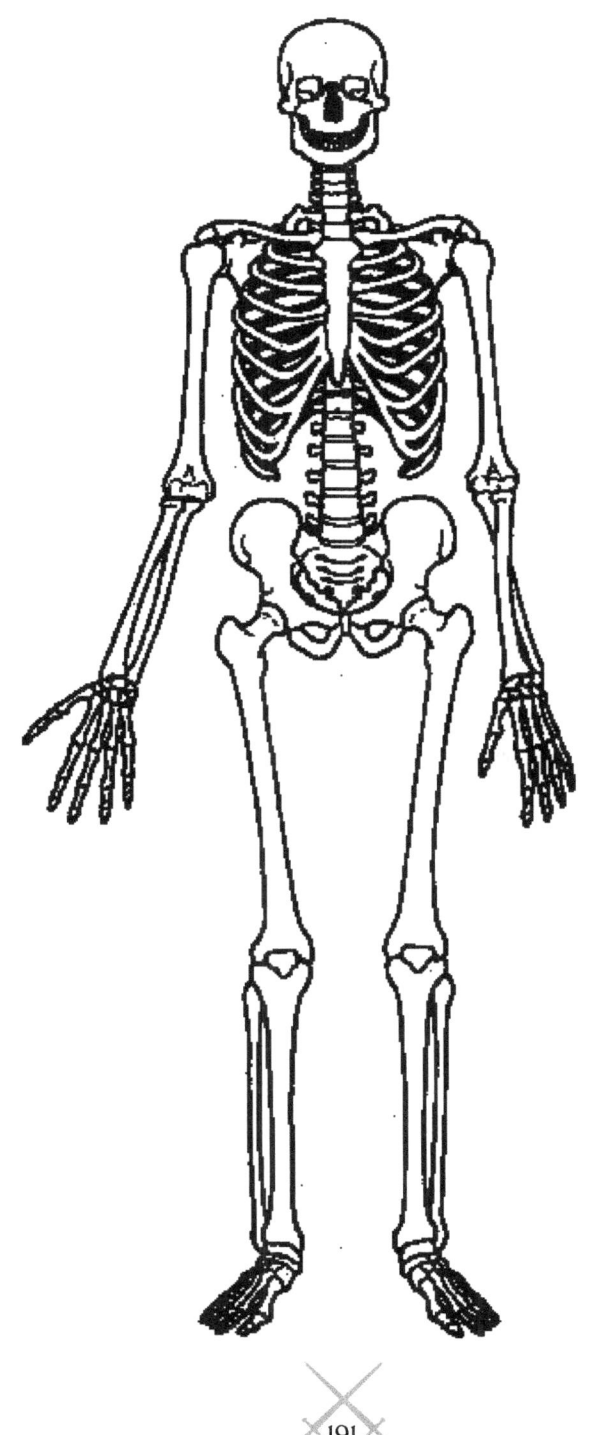

Where are the problems in your structure?
a)   b)   c)   d)   e)   f)

Now look at muscles, tissues, organs etc.
g)   h)   i)   j)   k)   l)

Make an inventory of problem areas. Like a builder ask: *"How am I going to fix this structure?"*

(4) How do you feel you can allow your High Priest masculine energy channel to flow through you? Can you "feel" when his energy has entered your body? What rituals do you use to get him inside you?

i.e. Breath; Asking for him to be present;
List whatever you use daily to get "him" to you.

(5) Who was the most heart-centered role model for you in your biological "lineage?" If you do not know this "ancestor" personally, feel yourself acknowledging him and drawing on his strength and creative heart. Look carefully at both your mother's and father's sides. Which side is most dominant?

(6) What did you feel when you looked at the right side of your face with the paper? What difference was there between left and right? You can take a photo to do this exercise as well.

(7) (a) Which parts of yourself do you have to forgive to help you in understanding yourself here?

(7) (b) Do you find it hard to surrender to these aspects of yourself?

(8) (a) Have you been challenged by another man since developing your relationship with your High Priest and if so, could you feel your High Priest changing the vibration inside you to respond in the way you "he" would in the situation?

(8) (b) Do you feel you can be responsible for this new self and what it will do to change your relationships?

(9) How do you feel about addressing the imbalances within yourself when confronted with the world "man" has made environmentally and with technological advances? What small or big things can you do to address these imbalances in nature?

(10) Do you find it hard to surrender to this new masculine force growing inside you?

(11) List strong, powerful, protective people in your life. How can you see the masculine working in their lives?

(12) Which place did you choose when you were invited to go on your tour to any destination in the world or universe? Was there any hesitation in choosing your destination? If so why? Describe what your heart needs to experience in this adventure.

(13) How do you feel about the ascension process with the High Priest? For example can you allow yourself a reality which sees the importance of being aligned to the "true earth?" Describe what the nature of "foundations" and being "truly earthed" is to you.

(14) Visualize now where you can actually witness a fruitful and pleasant outcome in the exercise by surrendering to the forces of the High Priest.

Lesson 4:

The Vibration of The High Priest

(1) In beginning your relationship with The High Priest, describe how you feel about expecting too much from this new relationship?

(2) Have you felt yourself expecting too much of The High Priest?

(3) When your heart chakra is opening to The High Priest you can experience many powerful shifts. What has been the reaction of friends, family, partner, etc.?

(4) Who has had to go from your life? List, and the reasons why?

(5) Can you now sense why you had these people in your life? (i.e. to fill an empty space, company, your own unmet needs, etc.)

(6) Which sentence resonates with you in your newly emerging identity?

I am now home.
I am on my own.
I am safe and free in the exploration of my masculine.
I am loved.
Why?

Were there any other feelings you would like to observe which have helped you create this shift in consciousness?

(7) (a) What do you feel The High Priest means when he says "all of life" partakes in the journey of The High Priest?

(7) (b) Can you see how The High Priest can help you fight for your "soul?"

(7) (c) In strengthening your own inner masculine can you see how the world we have (the patriarchal world) is released "energetically?"

(7) (d) Can you see why your culture or upbringing, etc. has denied you your masculine?

(7) (e) By being responsible for yourself, you are creating with the masculine. How do you feel about this "responsibility?"

(8) (a) Are you finding The High Priest strengthening and clearing your body from misuses? (i.e. change diet, exercise program, emotional excesses released through therapy)

(8) (b) In encounters with people, can you demonstrate that The High Priest has helped you change your encounters with people of both sexes?

(8) (c) How does it feel to step outside your cultural and social definition of yourself?

(9) (a) In visualizing the serpent exercise, (the Sekhem), what was your first reaction to the serpent inside you? (i.e. danger, fear, horror, fascination, other)

(9) (b) What have been your encounters with snakes throughout your life?

(9) (c) Do you feel ready to challenge your serpent power and become an immortal?

(9) (d) Can you imagine what may unleash if you open your own basket of fears? (i.e. anxiety, depression, etc.)

(9) (e) By having The High Priest in your life can you utilize him to keep the serpent "manageable: as you make your ascent through your energy belts to the heart center?

(10) (a) Can you be a witness to your emotions being your biggest barrier to your heart center? List emotions and observe yourself in witnessing them.

(10) (b) Can you see also that they can be your greatest power?

(10) (c) Have you ever attacked your emotions in such a way, unleashing your serpent, so you couldn't "control" your own emotional reactions in situations? (i.e. fights, rage, anger, violence) When have you "lost it" and why?

(10) (d) Our cellular memory carries triggers, which set us off. Have you ever felt a victim of your own emotions in this regard?

(10) (e) The High Priest integrates your energies. How do you feel he does this?

(10) (f) Are you able to discriminate and observe your own emotional reaction to the masculine expression in our society? (i.e. government regulations, banking laws, environment and political decisions in their unbalanced masculine energy)

You will need to go back over this chapter many times to answer these questions.

Lesson 5:

Your Creative Force

(1) "You become what you create." What are you creating now in your relationship with your High Priest?

(2) How do you feel about allowing yourself the power to bring truth to your life?

(3) (a) Why are men trying to destroy "what is within them" which is seen as their creative masculine?

(3) (b) What other men and women do to you is a reflection of what society pitches to them. How do you feel about this?

(3) (c) What is your definition of the "masculine heart?"

(4) In your "integration" of your High Priest have you felt any problems in your body? (i.e. lower body and base chakra)

(5) How does "All Love" support the merging of "All Life" through the masculine?

(6) The "universal heart" brings your masculine into alignment with your truth. Have you felt the sense of activation of the "universal heart?"

(7) Do you feel the mergence with The High Priest at any level in your identity? How has this activation taken place?

(8) You now need to sever all dark masculine forces, which work consciously or unconsciously through others to destroy the newly emerging masculine.

"I now forgive all aspects of the dark masculine which has tried to destroy my truth." This affirmation is the release. How do you feel about chanting this affirmation?

(9) You are being asked by The High Priest to give yourself a gift. It is the gift to yourself. The masculine is a gift to yourself. **What does this energy feel like to you?**

(10) How is your mind creating problems in your newly emerging relationship with your masculine?

(11) Now you are allowing yourself to fully embrace the creative masculine.

List your reasons for wanting the masculine energy.

Lesson 6:

Opening up to Your Consciousness

(1) (a) What did you experience as you opened up to receiving through the vibration of the creative masculine?

(1) (b) Are you experiencing a sense of peace and order in your world by acting lovingly toward your creative masculine? (i.e. new people in your world, old ones going)

(2) (a) How are the sun's powers having an effect on your power and life force?

(2) (b) Magical forces through magician Priests help create the potential of your humanness. **Have you experienced these magical forces operating in your life?**

(3) The Priests state "there is a sense of peace and wonder when you attune to their presence." **Are you allowing this attunement to take place and if so, what are the results?**

(4) Can you demonstrate where "intent" being manifested in your life has already had results in your life? (i.e. new car, business, relationship, etc.)

(5) Which part of "you" rebel when you feel challenged? (i.e. what emotional reactions are triggered, you need to find a solution, control outcomes, etc.) Describe:

(6) The exercise of holding the golden rope of the Buddha is an example of holding back the rampant mind. **Can you imagine yourself doing this? If so, what was the result?**

(7) As your consciousness opens up to "All Love" you will begin to experience your world in different way. **What are these changes and can you partake in any of these rituals?**

Lesson 7:

Universal Heart Frequency

(1) When spirit is being integrated into matter, what are the benefits for you?

(2) Have you begun to experience the "vigor, strength, vitality and powerful life-affirming energy" of your pure intent now?

(3) What will manifesting the energy of the Universal Heart Frequency bring you now?

(4) What do you feel when you visualize the "Sun and Milky Way" energy entering your energy field now?

(5) Have you begun any "Rituals of Purification" for the Divine Masculine yet?

(6) What benefits do you see coming to you from being in the presence of the Ancients?

(7) Are you feeling the benefits of "Power" from The High Priest?

(8) Have you begun to attract other magnetic beings to you in your new power?

(9) What is the most important thing these energies are bringing to you now?

(10) What benefits will you gain from being a Magician?

(11) Why does the heart have to be fully engaged for the process of manifestation to take place?

(12) How do you feel about allowing your own heart's chambers to reveal truth to you?

(13) What are the benefits of opening to this secret sacred part of yourself?

(14) What are the benefits of opening up to your truth?

(15) Have you felt the release of identification of every living thing that is not of the light?

(16) What is it that you must give yourself to receive the love that the ancient ones represent?

(17) "The power of the Sunrise" has benefits. What are they?

(18) "Feeling earthed is Magical." How is it making you feel right now?

(19) What fears are you needing to monitor in opening up to these new energies?

(20) Can you really believe in your new reality and what it is offering you right now?

Congratulations. You have found in these exercises access to a part of yourself you didn't know you ever had. It is a gift, embody it and love your new heart.

All Love and All Truth
Carmel,
Through The High Priest

ABOUT THE AUTHOR

Carmel Glenane B.A. Dip Ed. Owner/Director of Atlantis Rising Healing Center™ and Mystery School. Founder of the philosophy of The Divine Feminine in 2002 and Senju Kannon™ Reiki in 2008, teaches The Divine Feminine Mysteries through her Mystery School Ascension Training program. A powerful interactive and dynamic motivational speaker, channelled writer, esoteric teacher, and sought-after healer, Carmel is known for her transformative tours to sacred destinations such as Hawaii, North, Central and South America, Turkey, India, Bali, Japan, Egypt and the great central heart of Australia, Uluru. With more than 20 years in business in personal development, Carmel's intent is to allow people to receive through the Heart's Intelligence through the mother's wisdom.

Carmel is the Australian Ambassador for HappyCharity.org as Director of Happy Spirits. She is currently writing training programs for all of her books to offer her courses online to a worldwide audience.

Feminine energy teaching programs became a focus after 10 years of founding my business Atlantis Rising Healing Centre in 1992, which led me to spontaneously become a channel for "The Goddess of All Light," who guided me to establish "The Philosophy of The Divine Feminine" in 2001. Daily my consciousness is aligned to "The Goddess of All Light," where I receive written transmissions for my personal guidance and teaching.

Facilitating and leading my first teaching tour to Egypt in 2002; I have since taught in Egypt every year, as well as North, Central, and South America, Turkey, Greece, Hawaii Islands, Indonesia, India, and Australia. Each tour, book, and training has helped me "Earth" my body of Light; purging Earth attachments, as my ability to "Earth" (plug in) develops, holding more energy and light in my heart, for The Divine Ones to manifest.

In 2014, I was invited to open a Crystal Tones® Crystal Singing Bowl Sound Temple, and now incorporate these sonic Masterpieces into all my teaching programs.

I am in service to "The mother" and aim to have as many people as possible embody the teachings of our "Mother" through my books, teaching, and healing programs.

I am currently writing online courses to support The Atlantis Rising Mystery School ascension training program and creating new Guided Meditation mp3's to support the Ascension program.

About Lisa Malcolm Contributor to Part I Awakening the Intelligent Heart

Lisa Malcolm B.App.Sc. Lisa has a Bachelor of Applied Science and has been designing and presenting education programs within the university system for the past 10 years. She is an environmental scientist who sees that everything already exists for a truly sustainable way of living and to reach it we must make the journey into our hearts. On a spiritual journey of discovery from a young age, Lisa is passionate about the re-merging of science and spirituality and blends her backgrounds in both into holistic knowledge, research, and teachings.

To Connect with Carmel Glenane:
www.carmelglenane.com
www.senjukannonreiki.com
www.atlantis-rising.com.au
Ph: (+61) 0755 367 399

Recorded Meditations
By Carmel Glenane
featuring Crystal Tones Crystal Singing Bowls

New Dawn Meditation
By Carmel Glenane
Feat. Crystal Tones® Singing Bowls

Set Yourself Free Meditation
By Carmel Glenane
Feat. Crystal Tones® Singing Bowls

Core Identity Meditation
By Carmel Glenane
Feat. Crystal Tones® Singing Bowls

Today I am Receiving Love
By Carmel Glenane
Feat. Crystal Tones® Singing Bowls

Trusting to Receive Love
By Carmel Glenane
Feat. Crystal Tones® Singing Bowls

The Alchemies of Isis The Magician
Meditations
By Carmel Glenane
Feat. Crystal Tones® Singing Bowls

Embodying The High Priestess Meditations
By Carmel Glenane
Feat. Crystal Tones® Singing Bowls

The Immortals Meditations
By Carmel Glenane
Feat. Crystal Tones® Singing Bowls

Awakening The Intelligent Heart Meditations
By Carmel Glenane
Feat. Crystal Tones® Singing Bowls

The High Priest Meditations
By Carmel Glenane
Feat. Crystal Tones® Singing Bowls

The Miracle of The Mysteries Meditations
By Carmel Glenane
Feat. Crystal Tones® Singing Bowls

Embodying All Truth Meditations
By Carmel Glenane
Feat. Crystal Tones® Singing Bowls

All meditations are available on these and other fine retailers:

OTHER BOOKS BY CARMEL GLENANE

The Alchemies of Isis, Embodiment through the High Priestess By Carmel Glenane B.A. Dip. Ed.

Love fearlessly and passionately, for Love is timeless, infinite and unconditional!

Explore the Feminine energies with Isis and The High Priestess.

Carmel Glenane B.A.Dip.Ed. Author of several books on The Divine Feminine Mysteries has now combined *The Alchemies of Isis* with *The High Priestess* bringing readers the opportunity to embrace the secret wisdom of The Divine Feminine.

The *Isis* story is the story of all who love. Hope, restoration, and magic are yours when you lovingly embrace Isis in all her aspects. Every word brings Isis into your heart with "her" words of wisdom, power, truth and magic. Isis heals, restores, renews and resurrects new life; helping you open your heart to receive more love.

In the companion volume *The High Priestess* Carmel explores core issues in women's lives; relationships, intimacy, emotional love and spirituality in direct dialogue with *The High Priestess*.

You will receive Moon, Stellar (star), Nature Speak Meditations and Rituals for activating your 'Core Identity' to receive love, as well as lessons inviting you to deepen your relationship with your heart's truth.

"The Alchemies of Isis teaches us that every woman needs to be grounded and feel empowered, to be truly sexy and secure. I now feel both."

Dr Shelley Sykes
TV Host and award-winning author of Sexy Single and Ready to Mingle.

Awaken Your Immortal Intelligent Heart, A Blue Print for Living in The Now **By Carmel Glenane B.A. Dip. Ed.**

ISBN: 978-1-938487-23-1 (print)
ISBN: 978-1-938487-24-8 (eBook)

In Part I: DISCOVER THE SECRET POWER OF YOUR HEART'S INTELLIGENCE

New scientific evidence reveals that your heart has an important role in supporting the Endocrine function of the entire human body. Read more as Glenane explores spiritually and scientifically the heart's important role in activating the Mitochondrial DNA (MtDNA). Discover how your heart's intelligence can be activated by initiating your five primary senses. Learn how The Black Heart, brings primordial power, pure peace and acceptance of all there is.

If you have a heart, you must read, "Awakening Your Immortal Intelligent Heart"

"Carmel Glenane does a magnificent job to remind the world that the center of our life is found by living from the center of our heart. In a time where consciousness is often mistaken for the mind, or even brain activity, Glenane presents a daily practice of heart-centered healing where weaving science, ancient spiritual disciplines, wisdom studies, and exercises of activation, provides the reader direct access to deep, personal growth. "
~Brenda Littleton, M.A. Ed., M.A

In Part II: THE IMMORTAL WOMAN

'The Immortal Woman' can be read sequentially or by opening up to any page for her message to be reflected upon for your day and see what 'She' reveals to you for your journey right now. Close your

eyes, take a deep breath in, ask your question, then open the book up to a page. This book is your personal 'living guide' as the ancient secrets are revealed to you day by day. *'The Immortal Woman'* tests and challenges your previously held definition of Love and takes you to a space of truth for yourself where all of life becomes a multi-dimensional experience.

Carmel Glenane Training and Workshop Programs

Carmel offers training and workshop programs on the Activation of The Intelligent Heart in Australia and overseas.

Training programs are also offered for all levels of Senju Kannon Reiki™, through the Atlantis Rising Mystery School.

Carmel also facilitates tours to sacred destinations throughout the world. Carmel travels with Crystal Tones Singing Bowls and invites you to bring your own bowl to be a witness to your heart's remembering in all sacred sites.

If you wish to sponsor training programs please contact the Atlantis Rising Healing Centre™ office:
email info@atlantis-rising.com.au

For upcoming workshops or training locations or tour destinations please see our Website:
www.carmelglenane.com or www.atlantis-rising.com.au

TRANSFORMATIONAL TOURS

Carmel Glenane Tour Facilitator

EGYPT TOURS

The essence of Egypt is in aligning your consciousness to the Ancient Deities themselves. The Hieroglyphics of the temples reflect, through the reliefs, architecture and atmosphere the energies of the Goddess's & Gods.

Egypt feeds your soul. Imagine being initiated to the frequencies in the Kings, Queens, and Subterranean chambers also known as the Pit in the Pyramid of Giza. Reflect on the timeless wonder of the Sphinx, touching the stele at the heart of its initiation chamber between the paws.

Discover old Atlantis again at Sakkara, as the desert winds whisper their secrets. Horus the Falcon hovers as he guides you to his temple complex in Edfu, revealing the essence of order, protection, and freedom — the ancient Egyptians were known for creating order out of chaos. Float upon the Nile, which reflects the starry body of the Goddess Nuit. Re-code your cellular memory with The Great Father Osiris as he resurrects your weary spirit in this most ancient of temples complexes in Abydos, healing you by the green Osirian well, where the secrets of the Ancient Flower of Life can be revealed. Be drawn to the mighty temple complex of Abu Simbel where Ramses II and Nefertari's love was immortalized.

Allow our holy Mother Isis to enfold you in her wings of love as we sail to her sacred home on The Isle of Philae.

The magician High Priestesses and Priests of Karnak allow you to embrace your own magical powers in their home of balance and duality. Sekhmet the austere warrior goddess/mother of Karnak will receive you if you respect her power.

Explore where ancient rituals and offerings were given to the stellar forces at Dendara, home of the Hathors, Goddesses of Love and Pleasure.

JAPAN TOURS

Japan is a transformational, feminine and nurturing experience, especially Mt. Kurama known as the 'heart' of Japan. Mt Kurama, located 40mins outside the imperial ancient city of Kyoto, is the mountain where Dr. USUI received his enlightenment. Japan's delicate and very special spiritual energies reflect the beauty and power of Senju Kannon Mother of Japan and mother of our Feminine Reiki.

The Japan journey begins in the ancient shrine city of Kyoto, visiting powerful Buddhist temples, including Sanjusangen-do–The Thousand Armed Kannon Temple with 1,000 Kannon's (also known as Quan Yin) statues in the temple. The city's beauty is phenomena, featuring spectacular gardens, a geisha district, authentic Japanese cuisine, peace, order and tranquility. Unwind in traditional Onsen style bathing houses of warm mineral springs, relax in the peaceful retreat rooms or indulge in authentic traditional Japanese cuisine.

Our training program honors the Dr. Usui (traditional Reiki) but embraces 'The Mother' feminine heart of Reiki. Our programs are tailored to sacred sites and locations in and around the Temples at Kyoto and Mr Kurama. Travelling with our Crystal Tones Singing bowls magnifying and amplifying this incredible energy.

www.ingramcontent.com/pod-product-compliance
Lightning Source LLC
Chambersburg PA
CBHW071607080526
44588CB00010B/1053